T0306650

TREASURES OF THE GOLDSMITH'S ART

TREASURES OF THE GOLDSMITH'S ART

The Michael Wellby Bequest to the Ashmolean Museum

TIMOTHY WILSON & MATTHEW WINTERBOTTOM

ASHMOLEAN

Copyright © Ashmolean Museum,
University of Oxford, 2015
Timothy Wilson and Matthew Winterbottom
have asserted their moral rights to be
identified as the authors of this work.

British Library Cataloguing-in-Publication Data
A catalogue record for this book is
available from the British Library
ISBN 978-1-910807-01-9
All rights reserved. No part of this publication
may be transmitted in any form or by any means,
electronic, or mechanical, including photocopy,
recording or any storage and retrieval system, without
prior permission in writing from the publisher.

Published by the Ashmolean Museum,
University of Oxford
General Editor: Katherine Wodehouse
Designed and typeset in Spinoza Pro by Vermillion, Dublin
Printed and bound in Belgium by Albe de Coker

Frontispiece: *Communion flagon*, by Johannes (Hans)
Lencker I, Augsburg, *c.* 1625–30. WA2013.1.166, cat. 33

For further details of Ashmolean titles please visit:
www.ashmolean.org./shop

UNIVERSITY OF OXFORD

ASHMOLEAN

Contents

Preface

In 2004 Michael Wellby proposed to bequeath his amazing collection to the Ashmolean, an offer which the Visitors of the Ashmolean, the Museum's governing body, accepted in principle with alacrity and gratitude. He died early in 2012. On receipt of the collection, the Museum immediately set about planning a new gallery which would meet the aspiration, as discussed over a decade between Mr Wellby and Tim Wilson, the Museum's Keeper of Western Art, that the Wellby collection should form the basis of a 'little Green Vault in Oxford', echoing the spectacular prototype of that name in Dresden. With the generous assistance of Arts Council England's Designation Development Fund and the DCMS–Wolfson Museums and Galleries Improvement Fund, together with the Silver Society, the Schroder Charity Trust, and the Goldsmiths' Company Charity, the Wellby Gallery, designed by John Ronayne and project-managed by Harry Phythian-Adams, opened in summer 2015.

This publication, timed to follow as closely as possible the gallery opening, describes a selection of the 500 or so objects in the Wellby collection; it reflects a fairly early state of research on the collection. A complete, though summary and preliminary, illustrated inventory can be found on the Museum website.

Although Michael Wellby was at the time of his death working on an illustrated personal catalogue of the collection, little detailed provenance or other information accompanied the objects to the Museum. A complete and systematic catalogue of the collection will require detailed collaboration from specialist curators, collectors, and members of the art trade, analytical input from scientists, and much more extensive research on provenance than the Museum has been able to carry out in the time available. Objects of this sort are highly complex and have often been subject to modification and 'improvement' during their lifetime. Future research is likely to reveal complicated histories for some of the works included here, as well as others in the collection. The descriptions and attributions given here should therefore be regarded as subject to revision: the authors will be pleased to receive comments from those with information on provenance or opinions on individual objects in the collection.

Left: Detail of cat. 7

Although our abiding debt of gratitude is to Michael Wellby himself for his exceptional bequest there are many others we wish to thank. First of all to thank Michael Wellby's sons, Christopher and Nicholas, for making possible the transfer of their father's collection courteously and smoothly following his death and for their subsequent assistance and advice.

A special debt is owed by the Museum to Timothy Schroder, who first introduced Tim Wilson to Michael Wellby and who has provided the Museum with advice and expertise over many years. The glossary in the present book is based, with permission, on that in his 2009 catalogue of *British and Continental Gold and Silver in the Ashmolean*.

A preliminary Museum inventory of the collection was compiled in 2013 with the valuable collaboration of Anna Koldeweij.

Among our immediate colleagues in Oxford, we are especially indebted to Catherine Casley for constant support in a hundred ways. We also thank Angelamaria Aceto, Sue Barker, Daniel Bone, Graeme Campbell, Unity Coombes, Tim Crowley, Helen Duncan, Clare Hills-Nova, Kevin Jacques, Mallica Kumbera Landrus, Declan McCarthy, Jonathan Moffett, Caroline Palmer, David Provan, Amy Taylor, Sarah Thorn, Catherine Whistler, and Jon Whiteley. We are indebted to Katherine Wodehouse for her skilful editorial work.

The works were cleaned and conserved in an heroic programme in the Ashmolean's Conservation Laboratory in 2014–15, above all by Elisabeth Gardner, with the collaboration of Nicky Lobaton, and the assistance of conservation students Francis Galarza Rubiano, Tania Desloges, and Rebecca Pont. The photographs are by David Gowers and Anne Holly. We are fortunate to have had the benefit of the first fruits of what we hope will become a comprehensive collaborative programme of metal analysis by X-ray fluorescence conducted by Dr Kelly Domoney of Cranfield University.

The Ashmolean also thanks for help of various sorts: Ellenor Alcorn, Niels Arthur Andersen, Maria Carmo Rebello de Andrade, Johannes Auersperg, Dirk Jan Biemond, Michèle Bimbenet-Privat, Marian Campbell, Harry Charteris, John Cherry, Julia Clarke, Glyn Davies, Kenneth Davies, Godfrey Evans, Riccardo Gennaioli, Philippa Glanville, Isabel Silveira Godinho, Simon Goodman, Jim Harris, Stein Holm, Douglas Howden, Alex Kader, Jutta Kappel, Kirstin Kennedy, Lauren Kennedy, Timothy Kent, Martin Kiener, Erika Kiss, Alexis Kugel, Hanspeter Lanz, Charles Little, Stuart Lochhead, Darren Mann, Teresa Maranhas, Cristina Maritano, Tessa Murdoch, Per Terje Norheim, Wim Nys, Nigel Palmer,

Luisa Penalva, Jct Pijzel-Dommisse, Alvaro Pinto, Paulus Rainer, Ella Ravilious, Jan Ribbhagen, Ralf Schmidt, Karl Schönefeld, Elisabeth Schmuttermeier, Ralf Schürer, Lorenz Seelig, Maria Sframeli, Paul Taylor, Christian Theuerkauff, Eleanor Thompson, Dora Thornton, Holly Trusted, Nuno Vassallo e Silva, Jeremy Warren, Ulrike Weinhold, Paul Williamson, Hugo Xavier, Catherine Yvard, Heike Zech.

Many other friends and colleagues, including experienced specialists from the international art trade who knew Michael Wellby, have commented usefully on pieces in the collection or helped in other ways. We thank them all.

The production of this book has been sponsored by a benefactor who wishes to remain anonymous and by the Friends of the Ashmolean. The Museum is profoundly grateful to them both.

XA STURGIS, Director, Ashmolean Museum

Right: Detail of cat. 39

Introduction

Timothy Wilson

MICHAEL WELLBY'S BEQUEST to the Ashmolean is the most remarkable accession of such objects to any English museum since Baron Ferdinand Rothschild's bequest to the British Museum (the Waddesdon Bequest) in 1898. This book is intended as an initial presentation in print of a selection from the some five hundred objects in the collection.

Michael Wellby, born in 1928, was a member of a family prominent in the silver trade over several generations; he died at his home in Haddenham in 2012 after a long and successful career as a dealer and collector (fig. 1). The focus of his interest was goldsmiths' work and fine craftsmanship, especially German and Dutch, from the late Middle Ages through to the eighteenth century. Like most great dealers, he never really retired. His collection was kept in a special room (fig. 3) in his house at Haddenham, where favoured visitors could admire and discuss the objects.

Following a start made by his father and grandfather, Mr Wellby set aside from his firm's trading activities many of the most precious and interesting works that came into his hands and over the decades assembled an unparalleled private collection.

Left: See cat. 25

Fig. 1 Michael Wellby at work, 2006. Photograph: Lord Thomson

Fig. 2 Casket, the mother-of-pearl work Indian (Gujarat), the mounts by Pierre Mangot, Paris, 1532–3. Mother-of-pearl, silver-gilt, and precious stones, 29 x 40 x 20 cm. Musée du Louvre, Paris, OA11936 © Musée du Louvre, Dist. RMN-Grand Palais / Martine Beck-Coppola

Fig. 3 Part of the collection as displayed in Michael Wellby's house in Haddenham.

Objects of this sort, though they had been of intense interest to wealthy Victorian collectors such as members of the Rothschild family, were not high fashion in the art market after World War II. Expertise was confined to a small number of specialists and his sharp and experienced eye was able to recognise many major works which had been miscatalogued. He had great fun with his collection and used to speak affectionately of both his own and museum collections as 'the goods'. In his own draft catalogue of the collection he gives a sense of his enthusiasm:

> *The excitement of the chase is a huge delight. To go to a sale or another dealer's shop and find something great that has not been discovered by others, nor recognized by one's peers, that is fun. Also, with luck, to buy it and know there is a fine profit if you are right. Sometimes, of course, you get it wrong, and it's a fake or a clever copy, but, as my old dad used to say, 'If you never make a mistake, you'll never make anything'. So the love of the hunt goes on, never dull, never boring, though nowadays the extreme shortage of quality pieces makes the moments of success fewer, and an unusual or beautiful piece in perfect condition a great rarity.*

The greatest of his coups was made in the 1960s – a mother-of-pearl casket mounted in France in 1532–3 by the Royal goldsmith Pierre Mangot (fig. 2). He bought this for a relatively modest sum, partly because, though it had a provenance back to the early nineteenth century, doubts were expressed about its authenticity and condition. Michael discovered the Paris marks on it and it was subsequently sold to the Louvre for a record sum; he noted: 'I was made an offer I could not refuse. So, though I parted with this piece, the huge amount of money involved made the acquisition of many other pieces possible.' Characteristically, he added a quotation from Francis Bacon: 'Money is like muck, not good except it be spread.'

The main strength of the Wellby Bequest is in precious objects of continental European craftsmanship. Many pieces show their original patrons' fascination with exotic materials, especially those from the East and Africa. There are beautifully carved and mounted examples of semi-precious stones, of exotic shells and mother-of pearl, of coconut shell, ostrich egg, and ivory. This extravaganza of exoticism wonderfully complements the Tradescant collection of 'natural and artificial curiosities' as well as the Ashmolean's celebrated holdings of English silver from the Tudor to the Georgian periods, much of which shows a more restrained taste.

Above all, Michael knew that the Ashmolean has long characterised itself as a 'collection of collections' where the obsessions of the private collector have been exalted and the public-spiritedness of donors honoured since the era of the Stuarts. The Wellby collection is one of the most spectacular enhancements of this tradition in the Ashmolean's venerable history.

Fig. 4 Attributed to Girolamo Viscardi (active 1628), *The Museum of Ferrante Imperato in Naples*, 1599. Etching, 30.5 x 40 cm. Bequeathed by Francis Douce, 1834. Ashmolean Museum, Oxford, WA1863.6228

Fig. 5 Joseph Arnold (1646–1674/5), *The wholesaler and ironmonger Dimpfel Family's Curiosity Cabinet*, 1668. Bodycolour heighted with punched gold on vellum, 14.9 x 19.1 cm. Ulmer Museum, Ulm, 1952.2611. Photograph: Oleg Kuchar © Ulmer Museum

The *Kunstkammer*

Matthew Winterbottom

MICHAEL WELLBY'S COLLECTION of sixteenth- and seventeenth-century goldsmiths' work and mounted curiosities is in many ways a modern-day *Kunstkammer*. He often described his collection as a miniature Green Vault – a reference to the largest and most magnificent of all the surviving European *Kunstkammer* collections. Many of the objects themselves would have been included in *Kunstkammer* collections when first made. With this in mind, the new Wellby Bequest Gallery is a deliberate evocation of an historic *Kunstkammer* display. The objects are symmetrically arranged on decorative brackets against a green background in homage to the celebrated Grünes Gewölbe (Green Vault) displays in the Residenzschloss, Dresden.

Kunstkammer is a German word that has no direct English equivalent. It literally means 'art chamber' although in reality *Kunstkammer* collections were usually more than simply rooms full of art and many of the objects they contained would no longer be considered as art. They were a reflection of the Renaissance interest in the world – both natural and man-made – and man's relationship to this world (fig. 4). Like the closely related *Wunderkammern* (cabinets of curiosities), *Kunstkammern* first appeared in the second half of the sixteenth century and remained popular into the eighteenth century. Some of the great princely *Kunstkammern* and *Schatzkammern* (treasuries) survive in Vienna, Munich, Dresden, and Copenhagen but many of the more modest mercantile and bourgeois collections have long since been dispersed (fig. 5). The Ashmolean Museum is itself founded on the remarkable collection of curiosities assembled by John Tradescant the Elder (*c.* 1570–1638) and his son, John Tradescant the Younger (1608–1662) in the seventeenth century. It is therefore a particularly fitting home for the Wellby Bequest.

Sixteenth-century collections of natural and man-made curiosities from around the world reflected the recent discovery of the New World and the opening up of new trade routes to Africa and the East. John Tradescant the Elder collected plants, seeds, and curiosities during trips to Europe, North Africa, Russia, and the Levant. He was also able to acquire North American ethnographic material from early explorers of the Americas. The distinction between *Wunderkammern*, *Kunstkammern* and *Schatzkammern* is not always clear. The words were sometimes used interchangeably and similar kinds of objects could be found in all three types of collections. An ideal princely *Kunstkammer* would contain both natural (*naturalia*) and man-made (*artificialia*) objects. Natural curiosities might include exotic seashells and corals, fossils, minerals, feathers, horns, and dried fish, as well as stuffed animals together with dried insects and plants. Rare natural deformities and freaks of nature were particularly sought after; Peter the Great's *Kunstkammer* in St Petersburg included live human dwarves and giants. Mermaids, unicorns' horns, and griffins' eggs and claws were among the most highly prized *mirabilia*.

Artificialia included art in the conventional sense – paintings and sculpture, both modern and antique. There might also be *exotica* such as South American featherwork or Chinese porcelain and costumes. Scientific instruments, clocks, and automata (*scientifica*) were also an important element of many collections although these were often made to be admired rather than to be employed in serious scientific research. Objects that displayed extraordinary feats of technical virtuosity such as miniature carved cherry stones or finely turned ivories were also greatly admired.

Some of the most distinctive *Kunstkammer* objects were the curiosities and hardstone vessels in elaborate silver and gold mounts. Many of these were made of natural materials that were extremely difficult to carve and polish. These pieces therefore cleverly united both the natural and artificial in a single object and demonstrated man's mastery over nature. The ultimate creator was God but it was the stonecutter and the goldsmith who brought forth the natural beauty of the crystal or hardstone hidden within. Vessels made from rock crystal, colourful hardstones, coconuts, the so-called horns of unicorns, and other natural rarities were often believed to have miraculous healing or poison-detecting properties. Poisoning was a very real concern. The word *credenza*, meaning sideboard or buffet, is derived from the Italian word for 'belief' because this is where servants would test food for poison before it was served. However, it is clear that many *Kunstkammer* objects were made simply to be admired rather than to serve any practical purpose.

With their collections of natural and man-made objects, princely *Kunstkammern* sought to represent the universe and man's place within it. They were attempts to gather together all reality in miniature – microcosms of the Universe centred on the figure of the prince. They therefore represented the prince's dominion over both the natural and the man-made worlds. However, they were rarely attempts to gather together the entire natural and artificial world – the rare, the exotic, the bizarre, or the beautiful were preferred over the commonplace. Only the very powerful and the very rich had access to the rarest and most extraordinary objects. These collections were therefore clear demonstrations of power, wealth, and prestige. Their primary purpose was to impress and to astonish.

Kunstkammer collections were formed both south and north of the Alps, although as their name suggests, they were especially popular in the German-speaking world. However, the collections of the Medici in Florence and the Gonzaga in Mantua were highly influential. In Francesco de' Medici's *studiolo* materials and objects made from them were displayed according to their appointed place within the hierarchy of the cosmos. From the 1580s, the finest paintings, sculptures, and works of art in the Medici collections were displayed in the octagonal Tribuna in the Uffizi. Reflecting the increasing status of art in Italy, here the emphasis was on works of art rather than on specimens from the natural world.

One of the most important and influential collections was that assembled by Archduke Ferdinand II of Tyrol (1529–1595) in Schloss Ambras, near Innsbruck. Described in the Archduke's will as a *Kunst-oder Wunderkammer* (art chamber or cabinet of curiosities), the collection was arranged, like that of Francesco de' Medici, by material in categories derived from Pliny's *Historia Naturalis*.

Following Italian examples, the displays in Schloss Ambrass were also intended to delight the eye. Different materials and categories were displayed in cupboards with brightly-painted backgrounds. Gold objects

Fig. 6 View of the silver-gilt room in the Historic Grünes Gewölbe, Dresden Residenzschloss. © Staatlische Kunstsammlungen, Dresden /David Brandt

Fig. 7 Anonymous Netherlandish artist, *The Paston Treasure*, mid-1670s. Oil on canvas, 165 x 246.5 cm. Norfolk Museum Service © Courtesy of Norfolk Museums Service

were shown against blue, silver against green, while *scientifica* – clocks, automata and scientific instruments – were displayed in cupboards painted in a flesh-like colour. Unlike the Uffizi, natural curiosities were still an important element of the collection, although these tended to be treated as raw materials for carving into works of art. Using hired glassworkers from Venice, Ferdinand founded a court glass workshop in Innsbruck specifically to supply his *Kunstkammer* (see no. 10)

The Ambras Collection was purchased by the Archduke's nephew Emperor Rudolf II (1552–1612). An important and intensely committed collector, he moved the court from Vienna to Prague where he amassed a vast and extraordinary collection of paintings, sculpture, and other works of art. He invited artists and craftsmen from all over Europe to work for him in Prague. Stone cutters from Milan created extraordinary vessels from colourful hardstones mined in the Bohemian mountains. These were given elaborate gold and silver mounts by highly-skilled goldsmiths such as Paulus van Vianen (1570–1613) and Jan Vermeyen (before 1559–1606) from the Netherlands (see no. 23). The fabulous collections of Archduke Ferdinand II and Rudolf II still form the core of the Imperial *Kunstkammer* in the modern Kunsthistorisches Museum, Vienna.

First mentioned in 1560, the *Kunstkammer* of the Electors of Saxony in Dresden was the second oldest to be founded north of the Alps after that in Vienna. Under successive Electors the collection grew to be the largest and most magnificent of all the princely *Kunstkammern*. It has been known since the sixteenth century as the Grünes Gewölbe (Green Vault) owing to the malachite green paint that originally decorated the walls of the room where it was kept. During the 1720s Augustus II the Strong (1670–1733) commissioned court architect Carl Friedrich Pöppelmann to create magnificent new rooms in which to display the collections. Pöppelmann created a sequence of threatrical baroque interiors with objects spectacularly displayed against painted and mirrored walls (fig. 6). The objects were arranged according to material in rooms that increased in splendour and rarity until they reached the mirrored Hall of the Precious Objects. Here several hundred spectacular objects were displayed against entirely mirrored walls. In 1730 Johann Georg Keyssler visited the Green Vault and wrote that 'The Florentine Tribuna and what goes with it, perhaps surpasses the treasures listed here in value: however, it cannot be denied that the mounts and well-thought arrangement of the objects and the impression they make, are far more striking than the Florentine collection'.

Although Britain never had princely *Kunstkammern* to rival those of mainland Europe, important *Kunstkammer* and *Wunderkammer* collections were formed in the seventeenth century. That of the Tradescants has already been mentioned. In Norfolk the Paston family formed a large and impressive collection of goldsmiths' work and mounted curiosities that was displayed in Oxnead Hall. Part of this collection was depicted in a painting in the 1670s (fig. 7). On a more modest scale John Bargrave (1610–1680) of Canterbury assembled a small collection of curiosities acquired on the Continent that he housed in two small wooden cabinets. Highlights included a mummified Frenchman's finger and a fossil from Saumur.

The increasing emphasis on paintings and sculpture as symbols of high status first seen in the Tribuna in the Uffizi eventually led to the decline of cabinets of curiosities and *Kunstkammer* collections in the eighteenth century. Art and nature were no longer combined in single collections and displays but were increasingly separated into discrete museums and galleries. During the nineteenth century there was a revival of interest in the magnificent goldsmiths' work and mounted curiosities that had been made for sixteenth- and seventeenth-century *Kunstkammer* collections. Baron Ferdinand Rothschild assembled a remarkable collection of Renaissance goldsmiths' work in his Smoking Room at Waddesdon Manor in Buckinghamshire. Rothschild's collection was bequeathed to the British Museum in 1898. Michael Wellby's collection follows in this fine tradition.

Overleaf: Detail of cat. 46

Catalogue

I Objects of medieval devotion

Two panels

French, probably Paris,
c. 1340–80. Elephant ivory
each 10.7 x 6.4 cm
WA2013.1.4.2 and 2013.1.4.1

UNMARKED

PROVENANCE: Paris, Hôtel Drouot, 14 December 1977, lot 41

LITERATURE: cf. Randall (1985)

The panels are carved with scenes relating to the Virgin Mary beneath cusped arches. In the upper scene on no. 1, the Assumption of Mary; below, her Dormition (death): she lies in a bed; Christ, standing, holds her soul flanked by apostles. In the upper scene on no. 2, Mary and God enthroned. Below, the Funeral of Mary: a group of men carry a bier; right-centre a man tries to grab the body; left-centre he falls down, his severed hands attached to the bier.

Devotional objects carved of ivory, which was imported mainly from East Africa through Islamic-controlled trade routes, reached a peak of sophistication in fourteenth-century Paris.

The fourth scene here is an anti-Semitic story told in the thirteenth-century *Golden Legend* by Jacopus de Voragine: while the Virgin's body was being carried for burial, a Jewish priest tried to knock it over; his hands miraculously stuck to the bier and were severed from his arms.

A long slot and flower-shaped depression in the back of the panel on the left indicates that the panels originally formed part of a container for scales and weights, a piece of medieval merchant's equipment which doubled as a devotional aid.

Plaque, The Crucifixion

Probably France or Duchy of Burgundy, *c.* 1400
Silver-gilt with enamel
8 x 6.6 cm
WA2013.1.7

UNMARKED

PROVENANCE: unrecorded

The ogee-topped plaque is enamelled in translucent colours: the Crucifixion of Christ, between the Virgin Mary and St John. On the cross is a scroll with the letters *INRI* (*Iesus Nazarenus Rex Iudaeorum*, Jesus of Nazareth King of the Jews). Above are the sun and moon.

The enamelling is in the technique known as *basse-taille*: the metal has been cut away before the translucent enamels are applied, so a three-dimensional effect is obtained.

The object is likely to have been intended as a pax, for the priest and congregation to kiss as part of the Catholic liturgy. TW

INRI

2 Ceremonial mace or staff

Probably Bohemian, Prague, mid- to late fourteenth century. Jasper and red-yellow moss agate, silver-gilt mounts
length 47 cm
WA2013.1.20

UNMARKED

PROVENANCE: unrecorded

LITERATURE: cf. Hahnloser & Brugger-Koch (1985) nos 522–5; cf. Lambacher (2008)

Constructed from nine sections of faceted jasper and moss agate with beaded silver-gilt mounts between. The haft is octagonal in section and terminates in a diamond-shaped head cut with six vertical pointed flanges.

This remarkable object belongs to a small group of closely related jasper and agate maces that are thought to date from the mid- to late fourteenth century. Other examples are in the Kunsthistorisches Museum, Vienna, Kunstgewerbemuseum, Berlin, Galleria Estense, Modena, and Bayerisches Nationalmuseum, Munich. Their original function is still not certain and they have been variously described as heralds' maces, parade maces, and sceptres. That now in Berlin was for centuries in the Benedictine abbey at Werden in the Ruhr. It was believed to be the sceptre of Emperor Charlemagne (747/8–814) and was used in the inauguration ceremonies of new abbots. All the maces are made from beautifully coloured and patterned jaspers and agates that have been cut and faceted. The stones were probably mined in Germany or Bohemia. Although Venice was the most important centre for stone cutting in medieval Europe, the maces were probably made in Prague. During the mid-fourteenth century Emperor Charles IV (1316–1378) summoned foreign craftsmen to the city to cut and polish colourful hardstones from the Bohemian mountains for reliquaries, vessels, and to adorn the Chapel of St Wenceslas in the Cathedral.

Medieval lapidaries listed the supposed magical, medicinal, and religious properties and virtues of gems and hardstones. Jasper was believed to heal fevers, dropsy, numbness, assist in childbirth, and prevent nightmares. Agate provided protection from poisoning and scorpion stings and snakebites. In the Book of Exodus, jasper and agate were among the twelve precious stones that adorned the sacred breastplate worn by the High Priest of the Israelites. Their beauty and purity was symbolic of heavenly perfection: the New Jerusalem described in Revelation 21 has foundations and walls of jasper, agate, and other precious stones. MW

3 Drinking cups from the age of Dürer

Probably Nuremberg,
c. 1490–1520
Silver-gilt, height 35.5 cm
WA2013.1.17

UNMARKED

PROVENANCE: Mayer Karl von Rothschild (1820–1886); Frédéric Spitzer, Paris; Spitzer sale 1893, lot 1705

LITERATURE: Luthmer (1883) Taf. IVA; Darcel (1891) no. 5; Kris (1932) p. 8 (supposing the finial doubtful); Kohlhaussen (1968) p. 339 (as possibly nineteenth-century); Krautwurst (2003) p. 438 (as possibly by the nineteenth-century goldsmith Reinhold Vasters); Truman (2013) p. 65

Cup and cover, with embossed lobes and applied cresting, on three cast feet formed as travellers, reminiscent of the work of the Nuremberg sculptor Adam Kraft (*c.* 1455–1508/09). Finial: a figure probably representing St Martin dividing his cloak with a beggar.

Probably Nuremberg,
c. 1520–5, silver-gilt
height 37.3 cm
WA2013.1.18

MARKS: struck on both rims with what is probably a reversed N, the town mark of Nuremberg as used until 1531 (Tebbe *et al.* 2007, no. BZ02); nineteenth-century French control marks

PROVENANCE: Frédéric Spitzer, Paris; Spitzer sale 1893, lot 1707; Sir Julius Wernher; Sir Harold Wernher; Christie's, London, 5 July 2000, lot 50

LITERATURE: Darcel (1891) no. 7; Rosenberg (1925) no. 3712B; cf. Kohlhaussen (1968) nos 355–8, 367; Hernmarck (1977) fig. 65; Krautwurst (2003) p. 341 (as possibly by Reinhold Vasters); Truman (2013) p. 65

Double cup, with embossed lobes and applied cresting. Around the rim of the lower part engraved scrollwork with dogs and birds. Set into the top and bottom are enamelled roundels, probably nineteenth-century.

Double cups of this sort were often made to celebrate marriages.

Probably Nuremberg,
c. 1500–30
Silver-gilt, height 35 cm
WA2013.1.16

UNMARKED

PROVENANCE: Sir Julius Wernher, Bath House, London (by 1913); Sir Harold Wernher, later at Luton Hoo, Bedfordshire; Christie's, London, 5 July 2000, lot 51

LITERATURE: cf. Kohlhaussen (1968) no. 354; Truman (2013) p. 65

Cup and cover, on eight-lobed foot, with embossed lobes and applied cresting round stem and cover. Finial: a winged putto in Renaissance style holds a probably later shield of arms, *quarterly gules and or.* TW

Fig. 8 Albrecht Dürer (1471–1528), *Designs for cups from the 'Skizzenbuch'*, fol. 153 *recto*, *c.* 1501–25. Pen and ink on paper. Landesbibliothek, Dresden, Mscr. Dresd.R.147.f © SLUB Dresden / Deutsche Fotothek / Regine Richter

4 Mother-of-pearl pendant, *St George and the dragon*

The carving and the mount perhaps both German, *c.* 1500
Silver-gilt and mother-of-pearl, diameter across, 7 cm
WA2013.1.29

UNMARKED

PROVENANCE: unrecorded

LITERATURE: cf. Pazaurek (1937) pp. 25–6; cf. Büttner (2000)

Mother-of-pearl carving of St George, on horseback, attacking the dragon, which is being trampled by the horse's hooves; the princess whom he is rescuing kneels on rocks to the left. The scene is set within a carved garland and the background is a greyer layer of the shell. The carving is set in a twisted silver-gilt mount with a suspension ring for wearing as a pendant. The head of the princess has broken away.

Although it is not certain that the legend of St George the martyr has its origin in any actual historical person, the cult of the saint spread from the Eastern Mediterranean through Europe from the sixth century AD. The cult was further diffused by Crusaders who encountered the tale of the soldier-martyr while fighting against the Moslems. The story of how St George vanquished a dragon that threatened to devour a princess dates from the twelfth century. He came to be regarded as the patron saint of England from about 1350 following the foundation by Edward III of the Order of the Garter, but his popularity was Europe-wide.

Mother-of-pearl is derived from the iridescent shell of various marine molluscs and is found especially in species from the Indian Ocean, the Persian Gulf, and the Red Sea.

Carvings of this sort are usually attributed to craftsmen working in Germany; this was Michael Wellby's attribution for this carving and is that followed by most museums for this kind of object. However, it seems worth considering the hypothesis that at least some carvings of this type were made as pilgrim souvenirs, possibly near the Eastern Mediterranean sea-coasts, closer to where mother-of-pearl would have been obtained. Mother-of-pearl carving has long – possibly since the fifteenth century – been a traditional local craft supplying pilgrims in Bethlehem. TW

5 Miniature devotional book

Probably German, dated 1512
Silver, partially gilt
3.8 x 2.8 cm
WA2013.1.27

UNMARKED

PROVENANCE: unrecorded

LITERATURE: cf. Kohlhaussen (1968) no. 434

This tiny book is made of silver with some gilding outside and inside the covers. The covers are engraved with foliage. Inside, on silver pages, are eighteen engraved scenes from the lives of the Virgin Mary and of Christ: the Annunciation, bearing the date 1512; the Visitation; the Nativity; the Flight into Egypt; Christ preaching; the Last Supper; Christ praying in the Garden of Gethsemane; Christ before Caiaphas (or Annas?); the Flagellation of Christ; Christ beaten; Pilate showing Christ to the people (*Ecce homo*); Christ carrying the cross; the Crucifixion; the Lamentation over the dead Christ; the Resurrection; the Apostles taking leave of the Virgin(?); the Coronation of the Virgin; the Last Judgement. The book has two clasps and suspension rings top and bottom, as well as five fictive rivets on each side.

This virtuoso devotional aid is likely to have been made for a woman of wealth and status, who might have worn it hung by the rings from a girdle, rosary, or chain. The iconography resembles that of fifteenth-century German sets of printed New Testament illustrations. TW

6 *Memento mori* head

German, *c.* 1500–30
Elephant ivory
height 6.5 cm
WA2013.1.30

UNMARKED

PROVENANCE: unrecorded

LITERATURE: cf. Cologne (2006) p. 83; cf. Williamson and Davies (2014) pp. 471–7

Ivory pendant carved on one side with a dead man's face; on the other side a decaying skull with worms and other creatures. A scrolling band over the head is inscribed with a partially-legible German inscription, apparently: ... *iung und arm mein ellend dut...* (young and poor my misery...?). Silver suspension rings, top and bottom.

This bizarre devotional object is a *memento mori*, reminding the Christian that he or she must die, of an extreme horrific type reminiscent of some late-medieval tomb monuments. Beads of this sort were made as terminal pendants to strings of beads (chaplets) used by Catholics for counting prayers (rosaries).

Similar examples in museums are variously catalogued as French, Flemish, or German. The inscription here, though not fully deciphered, indicates that it was made in a region where High German was spoken; a very similar example with a near-identical inscription is in the Schnüttgen Museum, Cologne. TW

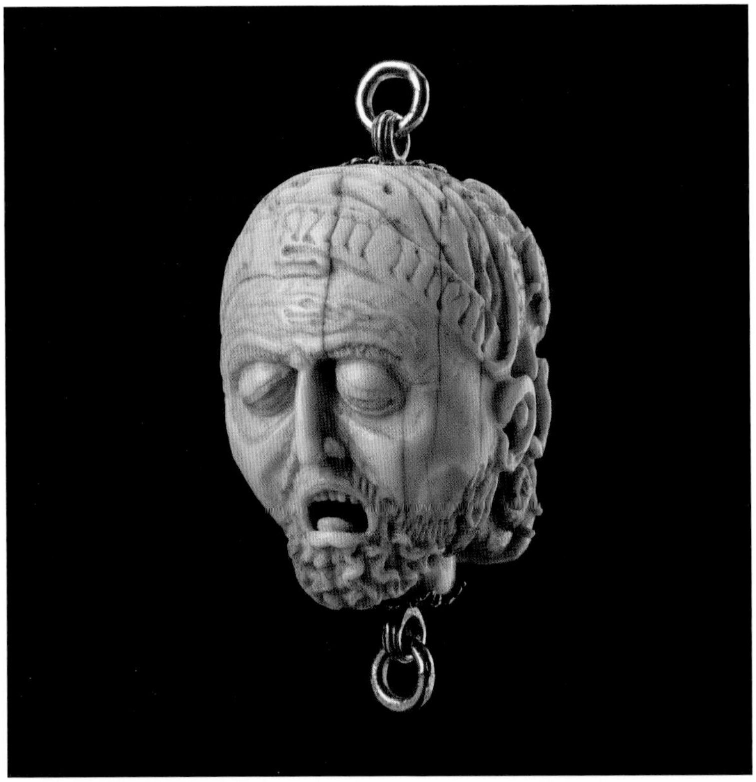

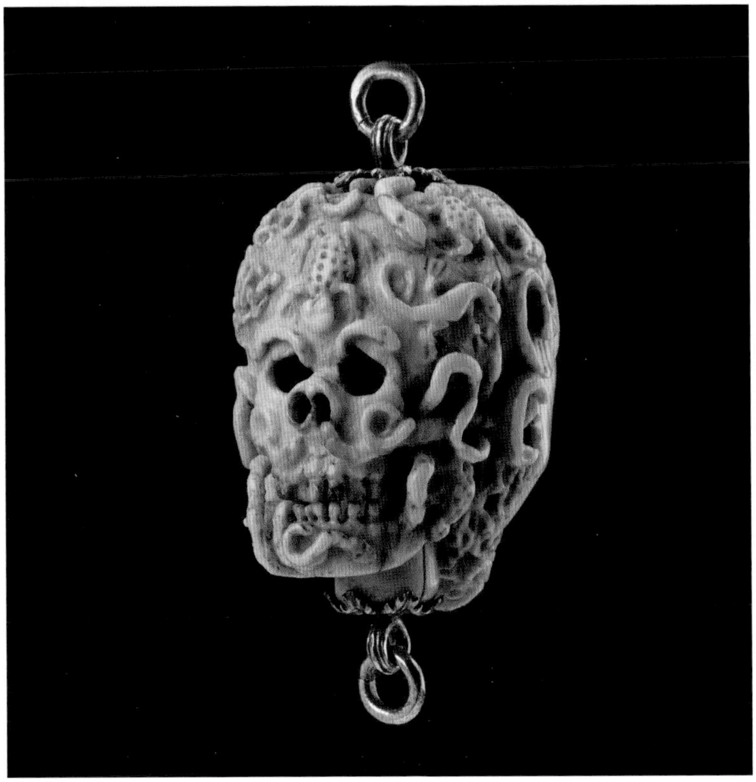

7 Ewer

Portuguese (Lisbon?), c. 1515–30
Silver-gilt, with enamel additions, height 43.5 cm
WA2013.1.41

UNMARKED

PROVENANCE: Joseph-Prosper-Gaetan d'Allinges de Coudrée (d. 1840), Cesare Alfieri; inherited 1840 by Emanuele Tapparelli, Marchese d'Azeglio; Christie's, Geneva, 29 April 1975, lot 109 (sold alongside the undermentioned basin)

LITERATURE: Robinson (1863) no. 1129 (exhibited with an accompanying basin, see fig. 9); Arundel Society (1869) no. 7; cf. Vassallo e Silva (2012) pp. 187–209; Warren (2014) III, p. 940; Wodehouse (2014) pp. 144–5

This monumental ewer, which would have had an accompanying basin for hand-washing at a court or aristocratic banquet, has cast and chased figural and foliate decoration on every surface. It dates from the end of the reign of Manuel I, King of Portugal 1495–1521, or shortly afterwards and is a quintessential example of the style named after him 'Manueline'. The handle is fantastically formed with monstrous figures, acrobats, and male and female heads; at the bottom are an artichoke motif and four heads above a basilisk. The spout, now truncated, is formed as a tree-stump with acrobats, supported by a sphinx-like male figure. The thumbpiece is modified from an Italian plaquette. Around the body and on the lid and foot are bands of figures including a queen with attendants apparently watching a joust, musicians, courtiers, horsemen in combat, frolicking fish-tailed centaurs and centauresses, monstrous figures, and naked men flaunting their bottoms. The main scene may represent an episode from some courtly romance or legend. An enamelled roundel of the Royal Arms of Portugal on the lid and the enamelled band round the neck are additions since 1975. Concealed beneath the band are undeciphered scratched sixteenth-century letters or symbols.

Manueline display silver, like some Manueline architecture, combines elements from the Gothic and Italian Renaissance styles and from Flemish art, such as the engravings of Israel van Meckenem, with elements from Portugal's Islamic heritage and from the lands, in South America, Africa, India, and the Far East, newly explored by Portuguese navigators. There is nothing in the art or architecture of any other European country that is so flamboyant, so richly-detailed, and so exotic. A ewer similar to the Ashmolean's example has been in the Portuguese royal collections since at least 1534, and is now in the collection of the Palácio Nacional da Ajuda, Lisbon. TW

Fig. 9 Silver-gilt basin, diameter 49.5 cm, which accompanied the ewer in the collection of the Marchese d'Azeglio. Photograph taken in 1862. Victoria and Albert Museum, Guard Book MA/32/14, negative 2906 © Victoria and Albert Museum, London

8 Coconut cup and cover in the form of a fantastic beast

Northern European, probably mid-sixteenth century
Coconut with silver mounts and later glass eyes
height 13 cm
WA2013.1.49

MARKS: assay scrape inside neck rim, otherwise unmarked

PROVENANCE: unrecorded

LITERATURE: cf. Fritz (1983) pls. 40, 51, 77b, 80, 95, 104

The body of the monster is formed from a coconut with three hinged strap mounts. It is supported on two cast front legs with claws and a long curled tail. An embossed mane of stylised curls surrounds the neck. The neck rim – revealed when the head is detached – is engraved with a band of grotesque ornament. The head has flared nostrils, elongated ears, and a pair of ram-like curling horns. The eyes are pale blue glass with black pupils. The mouth is open, revealing sharp teeth.

Of the nine coconut cups in Michael Wellby's bequest, this is perhaps the most extraordinary. Originally from the Pacific Ocean, coconuts were imported into Europe by the Portuguese from their colonies in India, Ceylon, and the Seychelles or by Venetian merchants via Arab traders. Known as India nuts, they were greatly prized as exotic rarities. Their size and shape made them ideal drinking vessels and they were widely believed to have aphrodisiac and medicinal qualities, including the ability to absorb or detect poisons. They were carved or polished and given elaborate silver mounts that emphasised and enhanced their value. These sometimes took the form of animals and birds – owls were particularly popular but eagles, ostriches, cockerels, and even peacocks are known. However, this cup in the form of an imaginary horned monster appears to be unique. The nut is set at an impractical angle to serve as a drinking vessel and the monster's open mouth means that the lid serves no practical function; in other cups the detachable heads functioned as smaller drinking cups. It was therefore probably a novelty to be admired on the table or buffet or in the cabinet of curiosities rather than used. MW

9 Cup with life-cast creatures and plant

German, Nuremberg, workshop or circle of Wenzel Jamnitzer, *c.* 1550–80
Silver-gilt, height 19 cm
WA2013.1.81

UNMARKED

PROVENANCE: Sotheby's, Geneva, 19 May 1997, lot 168

LITERATURE: cf. Pechstein (1971) nos 87, 155; cf. Hayward (1976) pp. 208–15; cf. Nuremberg (1985) nos 15, 513–16, 520–1; cf. Tait (1988) pp. 96–105; cf. Edgar Lein in Tebbe *et al.* (2007) II, pp. 205–15

Cup, six-lobed at the rim. The upper part is minutely cast with plants, insects and grotesque masks; the surface roughly finished and unburnished. The stem is formed as a female caryatid figure holding up the cup, which is held by catkins. The trilobed foot is set with intertwined snakes.

This fantastic object has generated divergent views. Michael Wellby, who regarded it as one of the prime treasures of his collection, believed the upper part to have been cast in a single casting, rather than with individual elements cast separately and applied. To some specialists, the caryatid figure, with its burnished surface contrasting with the rough texture above, has seemed likely to be a later addition; it (like the similar gilt-bronze stem of a mounted lens in Berlin), is a variant, on a smaller scale, of the stem of the monumental centrepiece, now in the Rijksmuseum, Amsterdam (fig. 10). The Rijksmuseum centrepiece, one of the great masterpieces of sixteenth-century goldsmith's work, was made by the innovative goldsmith Wenzel Jamnitzer (1508–1585) for the City Council of Nuremberg in 1549.

We owe to Darren Mann, of the Oxford University Museum of Natural History, the information that the beetle-like creatures on the cup and the grass-snakes on the foot are cast from actual specimens, respectively firebugs, *Pyrrhocoris apterus*, and baby grass-snakes, *Natrix natrix*. This extraordinary technique was a speciality of the workshop of Jamnitzer; it was adopted on a larger scale in glazed ceramics by the French potter Bernard Palissy (*c.* 1510–*c.* 1590). TW

Fig. 10 Wenzel Jamnitzer (1508–1585), Table Ornament, 1549. Silver, partly painted, height 99.8 cm. Rijksmuseum, Amsterdam, RBK17040

10 Glass and filigree tankard

The metalwork German, Augsburg, by Abraham Lotter I, *c.* 1570
Silver-gilt, height 20.5 cm
WA2013.1.82

MARKS: struck on the base with a pinecone, the town mark of Augsburg (probably Seling 2007, no. 6, as used *c.* 1560–70); maker's mark of Abraham Lotter I (Seling 2007, no. 740)

PROVENANCE: unrecorded

LITERATURE: cf. Hayward (1976) no. 494 (example in Toronto, by Lotter); cf. Schroder (1988) no. 132 (example in Gilbert Collection); cf. Schroder (2007) no. 58 (example in Schroder Collection); cf. Seling (1980) no. 133 (two examples in Kremlin, by Lotter); cf. Dresden (2012) no. 42; Seling and Singer (2007) no. 740

Tankard with hinged lid. A greyish glass cylinder is encased in silver filigree. Above and below, the silver-gilt is stamped with bands of strapwork; the rim, base, handle and lid are etched with moresques (heavily worn on the lid). The thumbpiece is formed as a naked male half-figure.

Abraham Lotter I was made a master in the Augsburg Goldsmiths' Guild in 1562 and died in 1612; he was the first of a family dynasty of goldsmiths in the city.

The etched ornament is of a type derived from prototypes from the Islamic world and described already in the sixteenth century as 'moresque', which was diffused across Europe by ornament prints and pattern books.

The glass is likely to have been made in the glasshouse at Hall in Tirol, near Innsbruck, which was run by the Höchstetter family from Augsburg and manufactured glass somewhat in the tradition of the fine soda glass traditions of Murano (Venice) and of Altare in north-west Italy. TW

11 Cup and cover

German, Nuremberg, by Christoph Ritter I, *c.* 1570
Silver-gilt, height 23 cm
WA2013.1.153

MARKS: struck on the lid and body with the letter *N* for Nuremberg as used *c.* 1569–76 (probably Tebbe *et al.* 2007, BZ07) and the maker's mark of Christoph Ritter I (Tebbe *et al.* 2007, MZ0728); maker's mark also on foot

PROVENANCE: unrecorded

LITERATURE: cf. Tebbe *et al.* (2007) I, I, p. 343, no. 5; for the medallion, Habich (1929–34) no. 2662

Cup and cover of elegant urn shape; on the cover a pinecone finial is supported by two scrolling brackets. On the body three masks are embossed in relief; the surface is etched with strapwork and moresque scrolls. Within the cover is set a later cast one-sided memorial medallion by Matthäus Carl inscribed *CHRISTOF:FABIUS. GUGEL. V.I.D.AET.55.A°:85.*

Christoph Ritter I, who perhaps originally came from Vienna, settled in Nuremberg and became a master in the Nuremberg Goldsmiths' Guild in 1547. He died between 1569 and 1573. He was one of the most successful goldsmiths of his time in the city.

Christoph Fabius Gugel zu Zelding und Lissbach (1530–1585/6) was a Nuremberg lawyer and town councillor; he married Martha Imhof, a member of one of the greatest Nuremberg mercantile and collecting families. TW

Fig. 11 Detail from no. 11 showing the memorial medallion by Matthäus Carl

12 Cup and cover

Dutch, The Hague, by Frans Arentsz. Bom (d. 1573), probably *c.* 1568–73
Silver-gilt with later enamel
height 30 cm
WA2013.1.79

MARKS: struck on the outer rim with a stork within a crowned shield for The Hague, the letter *R* (*c.* 1568–74) and a goat's head maker's mark, attributed to Frans Arentsz. Bom; with assay scrape and later control marks

PROVENANCE: perhaps made for Johan van Oldenbarnevelt; subsequent provenance unrecorded

LITERATURE: Pijze-Dommisse (2005) pp. 17, 18, 198, pl. 4; Koldeweij (2015) pp. 32–8

The shallow circular bowl and cover of broad, squat form supported on a baluster stem and domed circular foot. The surface is matted with plain undecorated bands on the foot, stem, finial, and the bowl and cover. The cover has a cast foliate rim and finial formed as a unicorn. Inside the cover is an enamelled shield of arms *argent a cross flory gules.*

Unknown to historians until its discovery by Michael Wellby, this cup is one of only ten pieces of sixteenth-century Hague silver known to survive. Michael Wellby believed the enamelled arms inside the cover were those of Johan van Oldenbarnevelt (1547–1619). A Dutch national hero, Van Oldenbarnevelt was a brilliant lawyer and statesman who played a key role in the Dutch struggle for independence against the Spanish. It has been suggested that the cup was given on the occasion of Van Oldenbarnevelt's marriage in 1575. The finial is in the form of a unicorn, a symbol of chastity and of faithful marriage. It may be intended to symbolise the bride, Maria van Utrecht (*c.* 1551–1629), who as the illegitimate daughter of Magdalena Jandr van Utrecht, was not permitted arms of her own. Unicorns were an attribute of the Virgin Mary. They symbolised her chastity as it was believed that they could only be tamed by virgins.

Despite holding one of the highest offices in the newly established Dutch Republic, in 1619 Van Oldenbarnevelt was tried and beheaded for his support of the Arminians in their religious struggle against the Calvinists. His possessions were confiscated and this cup is possibly the '*groote silvere cop met het decksel daertoe*' (large cup and cover) found sealed in a case together with other valuable silver in an upstairs room.

The maker's mark has been recently attributed to Frans Arentsz. Bom on the basis of its close similarity to that of his son, Arent Fransz. Bom. The Boms were a well-known family of goldsmiths whose name appears regularly in contemporary accounts.

Recent scientific analysis of the enamelled arms inside the cover indicates that they are of nineteenth-century or later origin and therefore probably later replacements. If they are intended to be the arms of Van Oldenbarnevelt, the enameller has mistakenly reversed the colours. They should show a white cross on a red ground. MW

13 Relief of *The Kingdom of Neptune*

By or after Willem Danielsz. van Tetrode (*c.* 1525–80)
Silver, diameter 30 cm
WA2013.1.111

UNMARKED

PROVENANCE: unrecorded

LITERATURE: cf. Scholten (2003) pp. 70–1, 124–5; *Burlington Magazine* 156 (October 2014) p. 719

Relief, embossed and chased with Neptune in his chariot surrounded by tritons, putti, fish-tailed centaurs, horses, a sea-monster, and sea-nymphs; dotted background.

An engraving published by Hendrick Goltzius in 1587, corresponding to, the same size as, and in the same direction as, this design, is inscribed *Guilelmus. Tetrho. invet.* (William Tetrode designed this) (fig. 12). Tetrode, who was from Delft, worked around 1545–67 in Florence, including for Benvenuto Cellini, and in Rome; he was one of the leading Netherlandish-born sculptors of the second half of the sixteenth century. It is possible that this silver relief, which has three-dimensional verve lacking in the engraving, is Tetrode's original version of the design; but one cannot, in the present state of research, exclude the possibility that it was made after, rather than being the source for, the engraving.

The broad plain border would have made this relief unsuitable for incorporation into a flat cup, and it may have been intended as an independent work of art for framing. TW

Fig. 12 Jacques de Gheyn II (1565–1629), after Willem Danielsz. van Tetrode (1525–1580), *The Kingdom of Neptune*, 1587. Engraving, published by Hendrick Goltzius. Bequeathed by Francis Douce, 1834. Ashmolean Museum, Oxford, WA1863.6605

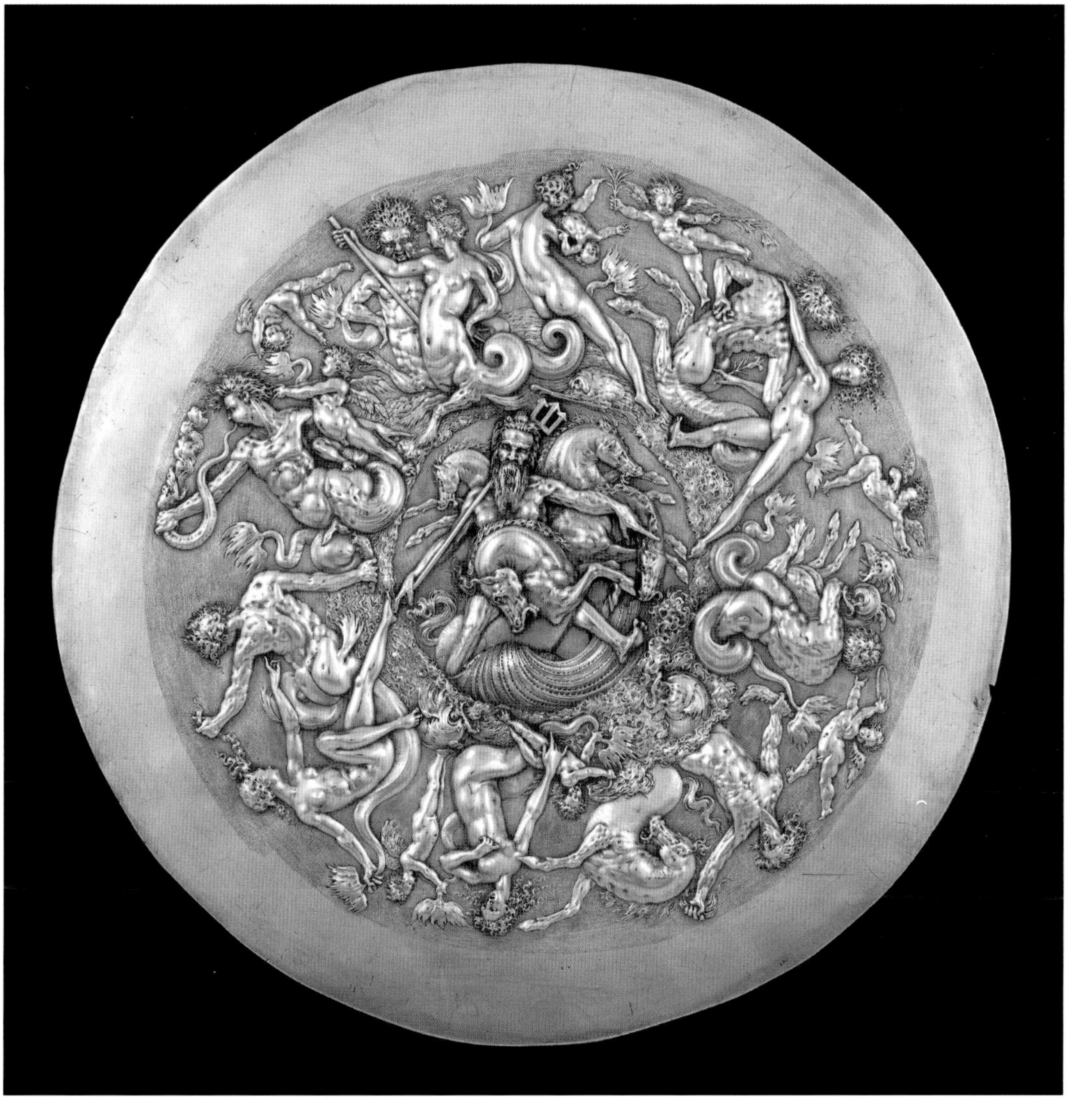

14 Ostrich egg cup and cover

Probably German, *c.* 1570
with later additions
Ostrich egg, silver-gilt, cold painted enamel, height 46 cm
WA2013.1.128

UNMARKED

PROVENANCE: Hamilton Palace, sold Christie's, 4 November 1919, lot 130; William Randolph Hearst (according to Christie's sale catalogue); Cécile de Rothschild (according to Christie's sale catalogue); Christie's, Geneva, 8 November 1977, lot 253

LITERATURE: cf. Hayward (1976) pl. 481; cf. Tait (1991), nos 3–4; cf. Tebbe *et al.* (2007), pls. 485–8; cf. Bock (2006)

Formed from an ostrich egg mounted in pierced foliate straps. The deep rim is engraved with masks within strapwork, and garlands of fruit. The domed lid has a broad gadrooned rim, pierced straps and a finial in the form of an ostrich holding a shield with a crowned coat of arms and the words: CHRIST BÁTHORY WAIVODAE. TRANSYLVANIAE. COMITIS SICULORUM 1576 (Christopher Báthory, Prince of Transylvania, Count of the Székely Land, 1576). Supported on a spool-shaped stem with embossed and stamped decoration and a domed foot engraved with strapwork and garlands. The engraved decoration on the mounts is highlighted in red, green, white, and black cold painted enamel. The egg and cover have an inner lining of silver-gilt with punched diapering.

Once believed to be the eggs of the mythical griffin, ostrich eggs were imported into Europe from Africa and Arabia. Others were laid by captive birds in royal menageries. Several were displayed in the Ashmolean Museum when it first opened in 1683 and cups survive in Exeter and the Queen's Colleges, Oxford.

The shield held by the ostrich finial implies that this cup was made for Christopher Báthory, Prince of Transylvania (1530–1581). It is dated 1576, the year Báthory was created Prince of Transylvania by his brother, the King of Poland. The Prince ruled Transylvania as a vassal of the Ottoman Empire. He was the uncle of the infamous 'Blood Countess' Elizabeth Báthory (1560–1614). Stylistically the cup would appear to date from around this time. However, the spelling of Báthory (rather than Bátori) on the shield suggests that the inscription is a nineteenth century addition or replacement. The band around the lower lip of the egg with pierced hearts and enamelled laurel sprigs and berries and the unusual lining inside the egg may also be later additions. It is not known whether the cup has a genuine connection with Christopher Báthory. Although Transylvania had a strong tradition of goldsmiths' work, particularly among its German-speaking communities, this cup was probably made in Nuremberg or Augsburg. High-quality goldsmiths' work from both cities was exported throughout Europe including to Hungary and Transylvania.

When sold from the renowned collection of the Dukes of Hamilton in 1919 the egg was painted with mythological creatures including griffins. The cracked egg has been subsequently replaced. The cold painted enamelling has also been refreshed. MW

CHRIST: BATHORI

15 Tankard with planetary deities

Mauritz Kaltschmidt,
Olomouc (now Czech Republic), probably 1579
Silver, parcel-gilt
height 16.2 cm
WA2013.1.150

MARKS: struck on the rim with later control marks, including an *F* for Brno, as used 1806–27 (Rohrwasser 1987, p. 11) and an Austro-Hungarian mark as used 1809–10 (Fromanger, and Diviš 2004, no. 562); control marks also on body and edge of foot

PROVENANCE: unrecorded

LITERATURE: cf. Luthmer (1883) no. 38B; cf. Richter (2005)

Tankard with a hinged cover. Around the sides are applied reliefs with cast figures representing the seven then known planets: *SATURNIUS* (Saturn), *IUPIDIER* (Jupiter), *MARS*, *SOL* (the Sun), *VENNUS* (Venus), *MERCURIUS* (Mercury), *LUNA* (the Moon). The cover is embossed and chased with masks and has a siren thumbpiece and a finial formed as a man in a curling horned helmet, holding a sword. Engraved inside the lid with a coat of arms, the initials *A.N.D.T.*, and the date 1579.

The seven planetary deities are shown with their 'houses', the signs of the zodiac which, in astrology, they are said to 'rule'. The figures are reminiscent of engravings by German artists such as Virgil Solis (1514–1562), but no direct graphic source has been traced. Another tankard, once in the collection of Karl von Rothschild, had the same figures on it.

Mauritz Kaltschmidt (d. 1580) was a successful goldsmith in Olomouc (Olmütz in German). Olomouc is in Moravia, now the eastern part of the Czech Republic. In the sixteenth century it had a substantial German-speaking community. This tankard is so similar in design to one marked by this goldsmith, published by Richter, as to warrant an attribution to him.

The arms inside the lid were identified by Michael Wellby as those of the Thomasis family of the Tyrol, which would correspond to the initials above the shield and is probably correct.

One of the control marks shows that the tankard was, in the early nineteenth century, in the region of Brno (Brünn), not far from where the object was probably made. TW

16 Standing salt and cover

Possibly Flemish, *c.* 1550–70
Agate with silver-gilt mounts
height 22 cm
WA2013.1.46

MARKS: partially obliterated assay scrapes on rim mounts to bowl and lid

PROVENANCE: unrecorded

The spherical salt bowl and cover are of grey-brown agate polished with polyhedral facets. They have cast rim mounts with bands of gadrooning and foliate collars at the joins with the finial and stem. The finial is a ball of agate within three grotesque brackets surmounted by a naked male figure with a winged sea monster. He is bearded and holds a short staff or club. The salt is supported on an oval stem of banded agate with vertical concave facets that sits on a cast gadrooned platform. Four slender scrolled and beaded brackets encase the stem. The circular foot is of faceted grey-brown agate with mounts cast with a foliate band of heart-shaped motifs.

Michael Wellby suggested that this standing salt was French but it is more likely to be of Flemish, German, or even English origin. Large and elaborate 'great' salts first appeared in northern Europe in the late Middle Ages. They reflected the historic importance and value of salt, an essential seasoning and preservative. In an age when poisoning by one's enemies was greatly feared, elaborate covers helped protect the contents as well as adding to height and general magnificence of the table ornaments. Tall standing salts were placed on the dining table in front of the most important guests; those of lower social standing were given simpler trencher salts. With the exception of Britain, the role and significance of the standing salt declined in the sixteenth and early seventeenth centuries. This salt is made from faceted and polished agate, a semi-precious stone that was greatly admired. Agate was widely believed to have magical properties including the power to render poisons harmless. MW

17 Ewer and basin

German, the mounts probably Saxony, perhaps Dresden, c. 1580–1600
Serpentine and silver-gilt
height of ewer, 28 cm
diameter of basin, 38.5 cm
WA2013.1.127.1 (ewer) and WA2013.1.127.2 (basin)

UNMARKED

PROVENANCE: Eugen Gutmann, Berlin (1840–1925); by descent. Restituted to the Gutmann (Goodman) family following World War II and sold by them in New York

LITERATURE: Falke (1912) no. 156; cf. Pechstein (1971) nos 81–2; cf. Hoyer (1995) pp. 80, 105, 128; cf. Syndram and Scherner (2004) pp. 198–205

Ewer, turned, carved, and faceted from a single piece of serpentine; silver-gilt mounts and handle. The curving handle is formed as a caryatid. The central mounts are cast or stamped with a repeating pattern of curling strapwork, grotesque masks, dolphins in high relief, and fruit; the foot mount has strapwork and fruit. The basin has a high central emplacement to hold the ewer. It is ornamented on the front with silver-gilt decoration attached at the back with floral nuts. Three of the panels have reclining water deities, two female and one male; three have masks, strapwork, and fruit.

Serpentine (serpentinite) is a stone, often variegated, which can range in colour but is most commonly of a dark greenish hue. It is soft and easily cut when mined but hardens on exposure to air. It has long been mined in the German state of Saxony and from the sixteenth century was especially worked into artistic forms in the town of Zöblitz, south-east of Dresden and not far from the modern border with the Czech Republic. Local serpentine, turned and mounted in precious metal, became a luxury product in which the rulers of Saxony took especial pride.

Ewers and basins, for which the prime function was washing hands at table in an era before forks were in general use, remained among the most spectacular products of European goldsmiths' work, even though this practical consideration lapsed during the seventeenth century. TW

18 Rock crystal bowl

Probably Italian, Milan, probably late sixteenth/early seventeenth century
Rock crystal and enamelled gold
height 12.8 cm
WA2013.1.119

UNMARKED

PROVENANCE: unrecorded

LITERATURE: cf. Distelberger (2002) nos 99–101, 107–10; cf. Krautwurst (2003) pp. 270–97, 452–87, 523–4

The ewer bowl is oval with gadrooning and a projecting front lip. The domed foot and C-scrolled handles are joined to the bowl with gold and black enamel mounts. The spreading foot rim is of textured gold with foliate scrollwork and ovolo borders in blue, black, and green *champlevé* enamel.

Rock crystal, a form of colourless quartz, has been prized since ancient times for its beauty and supposed magical properties. Its name, derived from the Greek word *kryos*, meaning frost or icy cold, reflects that it was once believed to be petrified ice. Some of the finest rock crystal was mined in the Alps. Crystals up to a metre long were laboriously cut and polished into vessels. In Renaissance Milan, rock crystal carving reached new heights of technical brilliance and complexity. The famed workshops of the Miseroni and Saracchi families supplied the courts of Europe with elaborately cut and mounted hardstone vessels. Venetian *cristallo* glass sought to imitate natural rock crystal but it was not until the invention of lead glass (or 'crystal') in the 1670s that man-made glass could rival rock crystal's clarity and colour. Thereafter the popularity of rock crystal declined until Renaissance revival pieces were made in the second half of the nineteenth century. Those made in the workshop of Reinhold Vasters (1827–1909) in Aachen are particularly convincing and can be difficult to distinguish from genuine sixteenth-century objects. MW

19 Tankard (*Hansekanne*)

Baltic coast, probably Lübeck, *c.* 1600–25
Silver, parcel-gilt
height 50.5 cm
WA2013.1.161

MARKS: Russian scratch weight or inventory mark under foot *N.21.4 ф. 92 зол*; otherwise unmarked

PROVENANCE: Shapiro Auctioneers and Gallery, Sydney, 9 July 2000, lot 13

LITERATURE: cf. Hasse (1965), nos 120–3; cf. Hayward (1976) pl. 531; cf. Hernmarck (1977) pp. 121–2; cf. Müller (1986) no. 41; cf. Tait (1988) no. 151

Tall flagon and cover on a broad domed foot. Embossed and chased with strapwork, cherubs' heads, trophies of fruit, and boar hunting scenes. With a pierced band around the body and an elaborate scrolled handle terminating in spiral tendrils. The cover is domed and has a cast finial warrior with spear and shield charged with two crossed maces.

Although unmarked, with its tall, narrow, outwardly tapering form and distinctive handle and decoration this tankard is typical of the Hanse tankards (*Hansekannen*) that were made in Hanse cities along the Baltic coast during the late sixteenth and early seventeenth centuries. The Hanseatic League was a commercial and defensive confederation of merchant guilds and their market towns that dominated trade along the coast of Northern Europe. Timber, furs, resin, flax, honey, wheat, and rye from the east were traded with cloth and manufactured goods from the west and herring and metal ores from the north. Large and imposing, Hanse tankards were popular with the city merchants who grew rich from this trade.

This tankard was probably made in Lübeck, once the richest and most important of the Hanse cities. Known as the 'Flower of the Hanseatic League' the city was an important centre of goldsmithing until its subsequent eclipse by neighbouring Hamburg in the seventeenth century. Similar tankards were made in Hamburg, Riga, and Reval (Tallinn).

The finial in the form of a warrior holding a shield engraved with the arms of the Dahmen family of Lübeck is a modern replacement. It was added after the tankard was sold in 2000 and does not indicate a historic connection with this family. It replaced a plain ball finial and is similar to a warrior finial on a Hanse tankard in the Thyssen-Bornemisza Collection, Madrid. The thumbpiece is also a later replacement. MW

20 Animal-shaped drinking cups

These amusing objects belong to a larger group within the Wellby Bequest of German drinking vessels in the form of various animals and birds. During the sixteenth and seventeenth centuries such objects were often used as 'welcome' cups for the entertainment of important guests. They were filled with wine or beer and guests would be expected swiftly to drink their contents. Owl-shaped cups were especially popular – there are three in the Wellby Bequest. In the wild, owls are often mobbed by smaller songbirds and so tethered live owls were sometimes used by hunters to lure other birds towards them. Owls were therefore symbolic of deceit and treachery. Owl cups warned the drinker against the 'deceitful lure' of excessive alcohol consumption. MW

Cup and cover in the form of an owl

Probably German or Swiss, mid- to late sixteenth century
Silver-gilt with glass eyes
height 15.5 cm
WA2013.1.72

UNMARKED

PROVENANCE: Christie's, Geneva, 13 May 1986, lot 42

LITERATURE: cf. Read & Tonnochy (1928) no. 69; cf. Hayward (1976), pl. 540; cf. Hernmarck (1977) fig. 191; cf. Fritz (1983) pls 39b, 40, 51, 77b, 81, 96b, colour plate 9; Nuremberg (1985) no. 52; cf. Tebbe *et al.* (2007) I, 2, figs 174, 179, II, p. 146

The raised body and detachable head are embossed and chased with stylised feathers. The eyes are inset with black glass. Engraved around the neck DRINK. AUS. SETZ. NIEDER. SCHENCK. EIN. FEILS WIEDER (drink up, set down, pour and repeat). The wings are separate and hinged to the body so that they can be opened and closed. The legs and tail rest on a cast circular base with an embossed and chased central putto's head surrounded by bands of strapwork with garlands of fruit and lions' heads. The foot rim is chased with dashes.

Cup and cover in the form of a tripping elk or buck

German, Augsburg, by Elias Zorer, *c.* 1605–10
Silver, parcel-gilt
height 27.8 cm
WA2013.1.157

MARKS: struck on the base with the pinecone for Augsburg as used 1605–10 (Seling, 1980, BZ26) and the maker's mark of Elias Zorer (Seling, 1983, no. 1019)

PROVENANCE: Possibly William Beckford, thence by descent; Dukes of Hamilton, Brodick Castle; Christie's, Geneva, 14 November 1989, lot 59

LITERATURE: cf. Seling (1980) fig. 149; cf. Tait (1988) nos 18, 19, 48

The elk stands with its front left leg raised on a domed oval base. The body and head are lightly chased to resemble fur. The forward pointing antlers are cast. An elaborate collar, decorated with quatrefoils and ovals forms the rim of the detachable head. The base is naturalistically chased with shells and foliage and has applied cast figures of a frog, tortoise, lizard, and crayfish. The underside is set with two applied shields of arms, engraved with a *fleur-de-lis* and a cow.

Cup and cover in the form of a bear

German, Nuremberg, by Christoph Ritter II, *c.* 1610–15
Silver-gilt, height 21.3 cm
WA2013.1.158

MARKS: struck on the neck and foot rims with *N* for Nuremberg as used 1609–29 (Tebbe *et al.* 2007, BZ13) and maker's mark of Christoph Ritter II (Tebbe *et al.* 2007, MZ0729); assay scrapes on neck rim and under foot

PROVENANCE unrecorded

LITERATURE: Tebbe *et al.* (2007) I, p. 348, no. 21; cf. Dresden (2011) no. 158

The bear stands on both hind legs with his front paws raised as if holding a staff (now missing). The body is expressively embossed and chased with fur. Solder joints indicate that the legs were made separately and attached. The detachable separate head is cast and of a thicker gauge than the body. The bear stands on a domed circular base embossed and chased with rocks and foliage with a plain foot rim.

21 Cup and cover in the form of a musketeer

German, Augsburg, by Christoph Erhart, 1595–1600
Silver, parcel-gilt
height 26 cm
WA2013.1.162

MARKS: struck on the base with the pinecone for Augsburg as used 1595–1600 (Seling, 1980, BZ21) and the maker's mark of Christoph Erhart (Seling, 1980, no.763) and seventeenth-century Strasbourg control mark (Rosenberg, 1928, no. 6951); assay scrapes under base and on neck

PROVENANCE: Baron Lionel de Rothschild, M.P. (by 1862); Leopold de Rothschild

LITERATURE: Chaffers and Robinson (1863) no. 6165; Jones (1907) pl. XVIII; Rosenberg (1922) p. 42, no. 129; cf. Seling (1980) figs 159, 164; cf. Tait (1988) nos 19, 20; cf. Christie's, London, 29 November 2011, lot 526; cf. Sotheby's, London, 6 July 2010, lot 2

Cup and cover in the form of a musketeer dressed in an embossed and chased jerkin, doublet and hose. His head is detachable and he wears a large wide-brimmed hat trimmed with ostrich feathers. He carries a cast flintlock musket over his left shoulder, now soldered into place. His musket rest and sword are detachable. He stands on a circular domed base, embossed and chased with rockwork and vegetation.

This splendid musketeer is dressed in the height of late sixteenth-century fashion. He appears to have been based on a print (fig. 13) from a series depicting officers and soldiers that was engraved by Jacques de Gheyn after Hendrik Goltzius in 1587. Particularly striking is his slashed and paned jerkin that is partly unbuttoned to reveal a peasecod doublet with its exaggerated padded belly. His shoes are similarly slashed. His fashionably long and loose hose were known as slops or galligaskins. In his right hand he carries a musket rest on which to support the weight of the heavy gun barrel when fired. Comparisons with photographs of this cup when it was in the collection of Leopold de Rothschild show that the current sword is a later replacement.

Christoph Erhart (master 1565, d. 1604) was a successful Augsburg goldsmith. In 1571 he was commissioned to make pieces for presentation by the Habsburg Emperor to the Ottoman Sultan. This cup was made only a few years before his death. Further pieces by him, mostly vessels in the form of animals and birds, survive in the British Museum, London, the Hermitage, St Petersburg, and the Hessisches Landesmuseum, Kassel. MW

Fig. 13 Jacques de Gheyn II (1565–1629), after Hendrik Golztius (1558–1617), *Musketeer*, 1587. Engraving, 21.4 x 15.7 cm. British Museum, London, 1864,1114.466 © Trustees of the British Museum

22 Mounted pottery tankard

The pottery Turkish (Iznik), *c.* 1600; the mounts English, London, 1607–8
Pottery with silver-gilt mounts
height 25.5 cm
WA2013.1.165

MARKS: London sterling hallmarks for 1607–8; worn maker's mark, a letter *R*

PROVENANCE: unrecorded

LITERATURE: cf. Atasoy and Raby (1994) pp. 270–1, pls 774, 775

Pottery jug, the fritware body glazed and painted with flowers in green, blue, red, and purple-black. The mounts and hinged cover are silver-gilt; the thumbpiece is cast as a siren with a cornucopia; the finial is in the form of an orb.

The double-domed part of the lid, including the marks, is unusually plain, though not uniquely so for a London piece of this date; it is possible the lid has been modified.

The greatest ceramic production centre of the Ottoman Turkish Empire was Iznik, formerly the ancient town of Nicaea. Despite the continuing state of war between the Ottomans and the European powers in the sixteenth and seventeenth centuries, East-West trade flourished. Examples of Iznik pottery that can be shown to have reached Europe soon after they were created include several surviving examples of jugs with London-made silver mounts. TW

23 Boat-shaped ewer

The carving probably Italian (Florence?), *c.* 1600; the gold handle possibly Prague, *c.* 1600–10
Lapis lazuli and gold
height 16.7 cm
WA2013.1.163

UNMARKED

PROVENANCE: probably William Waldorf Astor, first Viscount Astor (1848–1919); by descent at Hever Castle, Kent; sold Sotheby's, London, 6 May 1983, lot 292

LITERATURE: cf. Distelberger (2002) pp. 259, 267; Koldeweij (2015) p. 32; cf. Venturelli (2009) no. 30; Truman (2013); Wodehouse (2014) p. 155

The ewer is carved from two pieces of lapis lazuli flecked with pyrite. The foot, collar and handle are gold. The handle is asymmetrically modelled as a gracious boyish two-tailed triton with a horn. The collar and foot mounts are plainer and might be an addition.

Lapis lazuli is a mineral which was for centuries chiefly mined in what is now Afghanistan. In Medieval and Renaissance Europe it was especially valued and imported for use as the source of the highest-quality blue for painting. It could also, as here, be carved as a prestigious hardstone.

The Habsburg Holy Roman Emperor Rudolf II became famous for his interest in fantastical, exotic, and bizarre artistic creations and for his interest in science and the occult. He brought artists and learned people from all over Europe to his court in Prague. Michael Wellby hypothesised that the ewer was carved by Ottavio Miseroni (1567–1624), an Italian artist, trained in Milan, who travelled to Prague and worked for the Emperor. Mr Wellby compared the handle to the gold handle of a chalcedony ewer by Miseroni (fig. 14), which is signed as having been mounted by Paulus van Vianen (*c.* 1570–1613; see no. 30) in 1608, when Van Vianen too was working for the Emperor. Mr Wellby's belief in this attribution was reinforced when he took his ewer to Vienna for direct comparison with the mounts on the jasper example.

Paulus Rainer has, however, noted that the angular carving of the lapis lazuli is less closely related to Miseroni than to work carried out in the Florence workshops patronised by the Medici Grand-Dukes of Tuscany. The goldwork may nonetheless have been carried out in Prague; it can also be compared to the work of Jan Vermeyen, a goldsmith from Brussels who was, like Van Vianen, in the service of Rudolf II. TW

Fig. 14 Ewer, carved by Ottavio Miseroni (1567–1624), mounts by Paulus van Vianen (*c.* 1570–1613), 1608. Chalcedony with gold mounts, height 35.5 cm. Kunsthistorisches Museum, Vienna, KK1866
© KHM-Museumsverband

24 Standing cup

The mother-of-pearl work probably Indian, Gujarat; the mounts German, Augsburg, *c.* 1610–30, by Hieronymus Imhof or Jerg Hainlin
Mother-of-pearl and silver-gilt
height 18.5 cm
WA2013.1.125

MARKS: struck on the edge of the foot with the pinecone for Augsburg (worn), the maker's mark, either *IH* (Seling and Singer 2007, no. 1155, for Hainlin) or *HI* (Seling and Singer, no. 1351, for Imhof), and a later control mark

PROVENANCE: unrecorded

LITERATURE: cf. Schroder (2012) pp. 134–43; Wilson (2015) p. 8

The body and lid are made of joined curved panels of mother-of-pearl around a silver-gilt lining; on the cover and cup are twelve applied ornaments in the form of rosettes with scrollwork. The finial is a monkey. The stem is formed as a twisted tree trunk, with a squirrel and a parrot. The base is embossed and chased.

The construction of vessels out of small plates of mother-of-pearl pinned together was a speciality of artisans in Gujarat in western India. From the sixteenth century, the Portuguese began to import these objects, which were mounted up by goldsmiths in Europe; the 1532–3 casket illustrated on p. 10 is one of the earliest and most ambitious examples. On some other examples, the mother-of-pearl plaques seem to have been cut and assembled in the Indian manner by European goldsmiths.

Michael Wellby attributed the mark to the Augsburg goldsmith Jerg Hainlin, who became a Master in the Augsburg Goldsmiths' Guild in 1602 and died in 1630; but it could also be read the other way up, as the mark of Hieronymus Imhof (master *c.* 1620, d. 1635). TW

25 Three nautilus shells mounted in silver-gilt

The nautilus is a marine cephalopod, found in the South China Sea and adjoining waters. The iridescent, translucent, and geometrically satisfying shells were brought into Europe by the Middle Ages: an enamelled cover to a lost nautilus shell cup, belonging to All Souls College, Oxford, was made in Paris about 1300. The shells appealed to European taste of the sixteenth and seventeenth centuries: examples with elaborate mounts, often on marine themes, became favourite objects for princely *Kunstkammern*. TW

The decoration on the shell carried out in the Far East, the mounts perhaps Antwerp, *c.* 1580–1600
height 32.8 cm
WA2013.1.194

UNMARKED

PROVENANCE: Christie's, Geneva, 19 May 1998, lot 178

LITERATURE: cf. Tait (1991) pp. 68–87 (attributing an analogous object to northern Italy); cf. Mette (1995) pp. 75–94; cf. Schroder (2007) no. 64; Thompson (2013) p. 126, fig. 1

Shell, incised and painted with horsemen and plant sprays. Mounted in silver-gilt, formed as a sharp-toothed sea monster, on which rides Neptune with his trident. The hinged side straps are formed as climbing lizards, each with his tail round the head of the one below. The foot is naturalistically formed as a four-clawed bird's (eagle's?) foot. See p. 8.

The mounts German, Augsburg, by Ulrich Ment (active 1610–34)
height 36.5 cm
WA2013.1.196

UNMARKED

PROVENANCE: unrecorded

LITERATURE: cf. Seling and Singer (2007) no. 1237; cf. Rainer *et al.* (2008) no. 41

Shell, the mount with openwork pierced silver, parcel-gilt. On the hinged lid is Neptune in a chariot with three horses. Incorporated into the decoration are a dolphin, a lizard, an eagle(?), and a phoenix(?). The four straps are formed as grotesque caryatids.

Small shell, mounted in silver, parcel-gilt
height 32 cm
WA2013.1.202

UNMARKED

PROVENANCE: unrecorded

LITERATURE: cf. Repton (1844) p. 24; cf. Mette (1995) no. 23 (Rijksmuseum, Amsterdam: similar, but on a different foot)

The crane stands on one leg and holds a stone in the other. The upper part is chased to resemble feathers, the base as rocky ground.

Pliny the Elder stated that cranes stand on watch holding a stone, so that they wake up if they fall asleep and the stone falls; they were therefore regarded in Christian iconography as emblems of vigilance. The inventory (made no later than 1673) of the treasures collected by the Paston family of Oxnead Hall, Norfolk, included 'two shells fashioned like a crane, silver and gilt'.

26 Mounted nautilus shell

The engraving of the shell by Matthäus Merian, Frankfurt, 1632; the mounts and the ivory stem perhaps about the same date or a little later
Nautilus shell and silver-gilt
height 32.7 cm
WA2013.1.198

UNMARKED

PROVENANCE: unrecorded

The shell is engraved on one side with a harbour scene; on the other side, Tobias, accompanied by his dog and the angel Raphael, pulls a fish from a river. On either side of the back strap are engraved two women holding flowers; they flank a floral cartouche (now concealed beneath the strap), with the engraved signature *MERIAN 1632* (fig. 15). The stem is of ivory, carved with a muscular male figure, astride a dolphin. The mounts are embossed and chased, with a dragon on top above scrollwork with shells; on the front is a grotesque mask with marine trophies; the vertical straps are engraved with fruit and foliage; the foot is embossed with scrolls, cartouches, foliage, and shells.

The story of Tobias is from the Apocryphal Book of Tobit. Tobias was led by the archangel Raphael, in disguise, to collect money due to his father Tobit. When they reached the Tigris, a large fish attacked Tobias; Raphael told him to catch the fish and eat it, but to reserve the heart, liver, and gall. Later the fish's innards proved to have magical powers, protecting Tobias from a demon on his wedding night and healing Tobit's blindness.

Matthäus Merian the Elder (1593–1650) is one of the great names in the history of European book illustration. He was born in Basel and trained as an engraver. In 1616 he moved to Frankfurt and worked for the publishing house of his father-in-law Johann Theodor de Bry, for which he later assumed responsibility. His monumental series of maps and town plans, *Topographia Germaniae*, was frequently re-issued. No other example of engraved work by him on a three-dimensional decorative object is recorded. TW

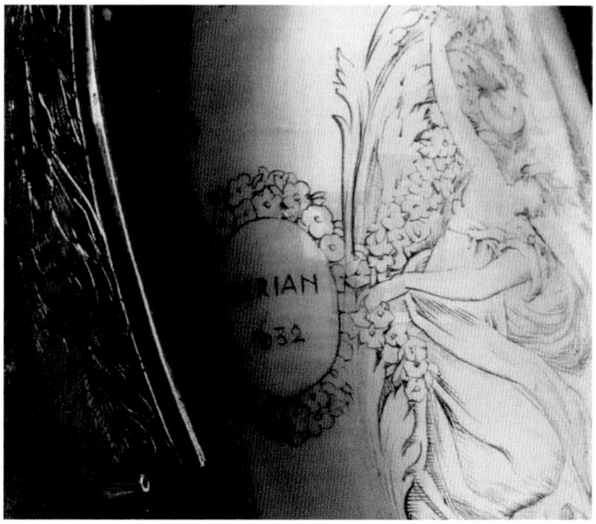

Fig. 15 Detail of no. 26 showing signature now concealed under silver-gilt back-strap

27 Standing cup and cover

German, Regensburg,
by Adam Seger(er)
(active 1597–1620), *c.* 1610
Silver, parcel-gilt
height 22 cm
WA2013.1.174

MARKS: struck with two crossed keys, the town mark for Regensburg (Rosenberg 1922, no. 440) and the maker's mark AS, attributed to Adam Seger(er) (Rosenberg 1922, no. 4456)

PROVENANCE: unrecorded

LITERATURE: cf. Tebbe *et al.* (2007) I, pls 440–4

The octagonal funnel-shaped bowl is flat chased with scalework and parrots within foliate scrolls and fruit. The cover is lobed and has a cast finial in the form of a musketeer standing on a ball with a foliate calyx. The cup is supported on a lobed baluster stem with a foliate calyx, scrolled brackets, and a shallow stepped foot.

Much of the German silver in the Wellby Bequest was made in either Nuremberg or Augsburg. This reflects the importance and dominance of these cities as international centres of the goldsmiths' trade. Despite this, most major German town and cities had their own independent goldsmiths' guilds and town marks. This elegant cup and cover is a rare example from Regensburg, an Imperial Free City in eastern Bavaria. Very little is known about the goldsmith Adam Seger(er), to whom it is attributed.

If original, the musketeer finial suggests the cup may have been a shooting trophy from one of the many shooting clubs (*Schützengesellschaften*) that existed across Germany. MW

28 Standing salt

German, Augsburg, by Boas Ulrich, *c.* 1615–20
Silver-gilt, height 21.1 cm
WA2013.1.171

MARKS: struck on base and under bowl with the pinecone for Augsburg as used 1615–20 (Seling, 1980, BZ38) and maker's mark of Boas Ulrich (Seling, 1980, no. 906); assay scrapes under base and bowl

PROVENANCE: unrecorded

LITERATURE: cf. Hayward (1976) pp. 238–9; cf. Seling (1980) figs 246, 251; cf. Nuremberg (1985) no. 21

The circular salt bowl is cast in the form of a flower head with a border of stylised petals or leaves. It has a chased and embossed outer sleeve in the form of a calyx. The supporting stem is cast and formed as a large spherical fruit balanced on the head of a standing ape or monkey. It holds another smaller fruit in its right hand and stands on the back of large stag beetle. The base is in the form of a heart-shaped (linden?) leaf, chased with veins.

German standing salts are exceptionally rare. In England large and elaborate salts retained their symbolic function and importance well into the seventeenth century while in continental Europe they tended to become smaller and more functional. This extraordinary example is marked by the Augsburg goldsmith Boas Ulrich (1550–1623). Ulrich appears to have usually specialised in silver mounts for the ebony table cabinets and caskets for which Augsburg was famed. This salt is quite unlike any of his other surviving work, examples of which are in the Victoria and Albert Museum, London, the Residence, Munich, and the Green Vault, Dresden.

The stag beetle on the foot of the salt is particularly unusual. Its startling realism suggests that it may be a cast taken from a particularly large natural specimen. A silver writing box by Wenzel Jamnitzer in the Kunsthistorisches Museum, Vienna, is similarly decorated with casts of stag beetles. The beetle's pairing with the primate that forms the salt's stem may simply be an amusing mannerist conceit with no symbolic meaning. However, in late Medieval and Renaissance Germany stag beetles were sometimes used to represent Christ through their equivalence with the stag – a holy animal symbolic of piety and devotion. Monkeys on the other hand embodied malice, lust, and greed. In their 'aping' of human mannerisms they represented man's desires unburdened by constraints.

An early sixteenth-century English salt with a stem in the form of a squatting ape survives at New College, Oxford. MW

29 *Nef*

German, Nuremberg,
by Esaias zur Linden,
between 1609 and 1629
Silver, parcel-gilt
height 39.5 cm
WA2013.1.173

MARKS: *N* town mark for Nuremberg (probably Tebbe *et al.* 2007, BZ13, as used 1609–29); a tree for Esaias zur Linden (Tebbe *et al.* 2007, MZ527a)

PROVENANCE: unrecorded

LITERATURE: cf. Nuremberg (1985) no. 108; Tebbe *et al.* (2007) I, I, pp. 256–8, probably no. 10; cf. Dresden (2011) no. 18; cf. Schroder (2012) no. 23

Model of a ship on an oval foot. The ship has one square sail and figures of sailors on the deck, in the rigging, and in the crow's nest; two cannons on the quarterdeck. The sides of the hull and the foot are embossed and chased with sea creatures. At the stern is a handle enabling the ship to be used as a drinking or pouring vessel.

Model ships of precious metal, known as *nefs*, were favourite centrepieces on royal and aristocratic tables in Continental Europe from the thirteenth century and throughout the later Middle Ages. They could have various functions – such as drinking vessels, containers for utensils, or salts – or could simply be ornamental. To some degree they fell out of princely fashion during the sixteenth century, but relatively modest examples like this were still commonly made by goldsmiths in Augsburg and Nuremberg well into the seventeenth century.

Esaias zur Linden came from Zurich. He qualified as a master of the Nuremberg Goldsmiths' Guild in 1609 and died in 1632. Ship models of this type were a speciality of his. TW

30 Ewer with *Perseus and Andromeda*

Dutch, probably Utrecht, workshop or circle of Adam van Vianen, *c.* 1620–30
Silver, height 23.7 cm
WA2013.1.182

UNMARKED

PROVENANCE: unrecorded

LITERATURE: cf. Hayward (1976) no. 638 (Rijksmuseum); Ter Molen (1984) no. 433; cf. Utrecht (1984) no. 65; cf. Van den Bergh-Hoogterp and Dubbe (1997) no. 25 (Utrecht); Truman (2013)

Ewer, raised, modelled, and chased from a single sheet of silver, with Andromeda beneath the handle chained to a rock. The handle is formed as a sea monster, the neck as a grotesque mask, and the sides as swirling vortices. In the front a lobed relief medallion, within an open monstrous mouth, shows Perseus flying down to attack the sea monster. The base is flat.

The picturesque story of how Perseus rescued the princess Andromeda from a sea monster is one of the most frequently portrayed subjects from Ovid's *Metamorphoses* in Renaissance and Baroque art (see no. 38).

This imaginatively conceived and fluidly modelled ewer is a delectable example of 'auricular' silver. A similarly conceived ewer in the Centraal Museum, Utrecht, is signed by Adam van Vianen and dated 1619.

The auricular style (so called because of a fancied resemblance to earlobes) was developed by Adam van Vianen (1569–1627) and his brother Paulus (see no. 23) in Utrecht. Adam's son Christian van Vianen (*c.* 1600/05–1667) came to England and worked successively for Charles I and Charles II. Michael Wellby thought this ewer 'probably by Adam', while Charles Truman has suggested it might be by Christian. TW

Fig. 16 View of no. 30 showing the chained figure of Andromeda

31 Columbine masterpiece cup

Germany, Nuremberg, *c.* 1640
Silver, gilded interior
height 19.7 cm
WA2013.1.188

MARKS: engraved under base with *225/39* and scratch weight *MI 8 ½*; otherwise unmarked

PROVENANCE: unrecorded

LITERATURE: cf. Nuremberg (1985) pp. 107–22; cf. Read & Tonnachy (1928) no. 103; cf. Tebbe *et al.* (2007) II, p.167

The lobed bowl is embossed and chased with auricular scrollwork, masks and cartouches that contain scenes comprising the story of Arachne; the Fall of Icarus; the Judgement of Midas; the Flaying of Marsyas; and two unidentified subjects. Figures of putti symbolic of vices or virtues have accompanying Latin inscriptions: *VIRTUS SINE FINE VIRESCIT* (Virtue flourishes for ever); *BREVIS ET DAMNOSA VOLUPTAS* (Pleasure is brief and destructive); *SUI AMANS SE PERDIT ET IPSUM* (He who loves himself loses his very self); *MEDIUM MEMOR ESTO TENERE* (Remember always to keep to the mean); *NON SORS: NATURA NEGAVIT* (Not fate but nature has denied); *TANDEM BONA CAUSA TRIUMPHAT* (But in the end the cause of good triumphs). Supported on a cast baluster stem and trefoil-shaped foot.

With its intersecting lobed 'petals', this beautifully shaped cup is based on the columbine flower (*Aquilegia vulgaris*). Since 1531 columbine cups (*Akeleipokalen*) had been one of the three 'masterpieces' that an apprentice goldsmith or journeyman was required to make and present before the Nuremberg Goldsmiths' Guild in order to become a master and be accepted into the Guild. The goldsmiths had to follow approved models kept by the Guild and they were required to make all elements of the cup entirely by themselves. Although the basic form of the cup remained unaltered from the early sixteenth century, the goldsmiths were allowed more freedom with the surface decoration in order to reflect changing tastes. This cup is profusely decorated with the fleshy auricular ornament introduced by the Van Vianen family in the 1610s but which remained fashionable in Nuremberg into the 1640s. Like this example, many columbine cups were not hallmarked because they were not intended for sale. The superb quality of the embossed and chased decoration indicates a particularly accomplished maker. A virtually identical columbine cup in the British Museum, London is embossed and chased with the same scenes and auricular ornament. Both makers probably knew each other as members of the close-knit community of goldsmiths. MW

SUI AMANS SE PERDIT ET

32 Windmill cup

Dutch, Nijmegen, probably by Hendrick Grondt (active *c.* 1625–51)
Silver-gilt, height 27.2 cm
WA2013.1.217

MARKS: maker's mark *HG* struck on edge of cup

PROVENANCE: unrecorded

LITERATURE: Koldeweij (2015) p. 34; cf. Nijmegen (1983) pp. 42, 66–7; cf. Nys (2012) pp. 61–2

Model windmill, with four sails which rotate and turn a dial from one to twelve when you blow through a pipe. Next to the pipe is a ladder on which stand three men, one smoking. In the sides are two windows, each with a figure looking out. On the top is a flag. The base of the windmill, when reversed, forms a drinking cup with three rings suspended from applied grotesque masks. The exterior is engraved with strapwork, flowers and fruit, and two shields of arms. The gilding may be later.

Cups made in the form of windmills were a novelty item made especially in Germany and the Netherlands from the sixteenth century. They were the basis of a drinking game designed to result in rapid inebriation. The drinker filled the cup and blew down the blowpipe; this turned the sails of the windmill and the contents of the cup then had to be consumed before the sails stopped moving. If he failed to do this, the drinker had to imbibe a number of additional cupfuls, as indicated by the number on the dial.

The arms were identified by Michael Wellby as those of Hertog of Holland impaling Van den Borch of Gelderland, and a second, later shield, with crown and supporters, which is for Menthen of Gelderland. TW

Fig. 17 Detail of no. 32 showing figures climbing up to and emerging from the windmill

33 Communion flagon

German, Augsburg, by Johannes (Hans) Lencker I (1573–1637), *c.* 1625–30
Silver, parcel-gilt
height 44.5 cm
WA2013.1.166

MARKS: struck on the foot rim, lid rim and beneath the spout with the pinecone for Augsburg, *c.* 1625–30 (Seling, 1980, probably nos 51 or 55) and maker's mark of Johannes Lencker (Seling, 1980, no. 1157d). Assay scrapes under foot and lid rims. Engraved under the body *K.z.E.* for Kirche zu Eisenberg

PROVENANCE: Stadtkirche St Peter, Eisenberg; Baron Karl von Rothschild by 1883; Daguerre, Hôtel Drouot, 14 December 2001, lot 40

LITERATURE: Luthmer (1883) no. 3; Lehfeldt (1888) p. 198; Rosenberg (1922) no. 456 d; Richter (1983) p. 29; cf. Tait (1988) no. 50; cf. von Falke (1928)

Pear-shaped flagon on a domed foot, embossed and chased with winged cherubs' heads, garlands of fruit and oval panels showing the Last Supper, the Crucifixion with St Mary and St John, and the Resurrection. The cast spout is in the form of an espagnolette. The hinged lid is raised in three tiers with a finial in the form of a pelican in her piety feeding her three young. Cast harp-shaped handle with scrolls and beading with the thumbpiece in the form of a cherub.

Formerly in the Lutheran Stadtkirche St Peter in Eisenberg in Thuringia, Central Germany, this large flagon was made to hold communion wine. The Eucharist or Holy Communion is the liturgical commemoration of the Last Supper. Lutherans, like other Protestants, allowed the entire congregation to receive the bread and the wine during the ceremony (*Abendsmahl*) rather than just the priest. As in England, large silver flagons were made in which to store the wine before it was poured into smaller chalices or communion cups. This outstanding example is one of the most splendid and richly decorated of its type. The figure on the cover of a pelican plucking at her own breast in order to draw blood for the nurture of her young is symbolic of Christ's sacrifice. This reflects the belief outlined in the Lutheran Confessions in the sacramental union (consubstantiation) – that the body and blood of Christ are 'truly and substantially present in, with and under the forms' of the consecrated bread and wine.

The flagon was probably made in the late 1620s for the new High Altar of the Stadtkirche. Completed in 1629, the altar was painted by Samuel Claus and, like the front panel on the flagon, shows the Christ and the Apostles at the Last Supper. Johannes (Hans) Lencker I (master 1602) was a successful Augsburg goldsmith who supplied both secular and religious plate. In 1626 he made a remarkably plain communion flagon for the Lutheran church of St Anna in Augsburg. Other works by him survive in the Residence, Munich, the Dommuseum, Salzburg, the British Museum, London, the Rijksmuseum, Amsterdam, and the Kremlin, Moscow. MW

34 Virgin and Child

Flemish, Malines,
by Maria Faydherbe
(1587–1643)
c. 1630–40
Boxwood, silver-gilt mounts
height 16 cm
WA2013.1.209

UNMARKED

PROVENANCE: unrecorded

LITERATURE: Trusted (2014) p. 105

The Virgin wears an elaborately draped robe, cloak and headdress and a silver-gilt crown. She stands on an octagonal base with silver-gilt mounts. She supports the naked Child, who has a silver-gilt halo and stands on an architectural pillar carved with cherubs.

This charming sculpture was recognised by Michael Wellby as the work of Maria Faydherbe, a seventeenth-century sculptor who worked in Mechelen (Malines), then part of the Spanish Netherlands. It is one of only a handful of pieces known to be by her and is one of the earliest objects in the Ashmolean by a known woman artist. The attribution is based on the group's close similarity with another of the same composition formerly in the Van Nuffel-Desmedt Collection, Antwerp, that is signed *MARIA FAYDHERBE ME FECIT*. A third signed Virgin and Child, in a Belgian private collection, is of a different composition but the Virgin similarly wears a silver crown.

Seventeenth-century women sculptors were highly unusual and little is known about the training of Maria Faydherbe. The daughter of a brewer, she was one of three siblings who all became sculptors. She was also the aunt of the better-known sculptor Lucas Faydherbe (1617–1697). She does not appear to have been a member of the Mechelen Guild of St Luke, which included artists and sculptors. Indeed, in 1632 she publicly complained about the Guild members' lack of skill compared with her own. She appears to have specialised in small-scale devotional figures of the Virgin and Child and helped to create a new Baroque style in Mechelen. MW

35 Pomanders

Sweet smelling pomanders were carried to ward off the foul odours and miasmas that were thought to cause the plague and other diseases. Their name derives from the French *pomme d'ambre* meaning 'apple of amber' because they were originally balls of ambergris and musk mixed with fragrant resins, spices, herbs, and oils. Early recipes and treatises list over 90 different constituent ingredients for pomanders. Many of these were expensive rare commodities imported from far overseas. Those most regularly used were benzoin, sandalwood, rose, labdanum, musk, nutmeg, ambergris, and cloves. The European centre of the spice trade was Venice, whose merchants traded aromatics from the Near and Far East.

Silver pomanders that open in sections, rather like an orange, first appeared in the fourteenth century. Different aromatics were housed in the individual numbered segments. They would have been hung on decorative chains around the neck or suspended from belts and girdles. The engraved decoration on the smaller pomander has been decoratively filled and highlighted with black mastic, itself a highly-scented resin from the Mediterranean. MW

Pomander and vinaigrette

Probably Dutch, first half seventeenth century
Silver, parcel-gilt,
height 6.1 cm (excluding suspension ring)
WA2013.1.306.5

UNMARKED

PROVENANCE: unrecorded

LITERATURE: Koldeweij (2015) p. 34, cf. Smollich (1983); cf. Schiedlausky (1985)

Spherical body with a screw top, suspension ring, and a high domed foot. Engraved on the top with rose petals and around the body with roundels representing personifications of Air, Water, and Plenty interspersed with fruits and leaves. When the top is unscrewed, the body opens in six sections, each hinged from the base, to reveal a central shaft. Each section is a sliding cover. Underneath the foot is a vinaigrette with a pierced and gilt grille.

Pomander

Probably Dutch, first half seventeenth century
Silver with mastic
height 5.5 cm (excluding suspension ring)
WA2013.1.305.2

UNMARKED

PROVENANCE: unrecorded

LITERATURE: Koldeweij (2015) p. 34, cf. Smollich (1983); cf. Schiedlausky (1985)

Ovoid body with a screw top and suspension ring and pierced domed foot. Engraved with designs of birds and flowers within foliate scrolls which have been partially filled with black mastic. When the top is unscrewed, the body opens in six sections, each hinged from the base, to reveal a central shaft. Each section has a sliding cover.

36 Beakers

There are over 80 beakers in Michael Wellby's bequest and they are the most numerous type of object that he collected. Most were made in the Netherlands, the German-speaking lands, and Scandinavia and range in date from the sixteenth to the eighteenth centuries. Beakers were used as personal drinking vessels for beer or wine. Their small size made them relatively affordable and, together with spoons, they might be the only items of silver owned by more modest households. Like spoons they were also given as christening and wedding gifts.

Silver beakers were made across Europe in a wide variety of shapes and styles over many centuries. Here two of the beakers cleverly imitate everyday beakers made of more humble wood and forest glass. MW

Beaker (roemer)

German, Nuremberg,
by Hieronymus Peller
(*c.* 1633–1686), *c.* 1670–3
Silver, parcel-gilt
height 6.8 cm
WA2013.1.103.1

MARKS: struck under foot with the letter N for Nuremberg, 1670–3 (Tebbe *et al.* 2007, BZ24) and maker's mark of Hieronymus Peller (Tebbe *et al.* 2007, MZ0634); with assay scrape

PROVENANCE: unrecorded

LITERATURE: Tebbe *et al.* (2007) no. 634.14

In the form of an octagonal glass roemer on a drum-shaped stem/foot embossed with scallop-like 'prunts'. The body is engraved with individual tulips. Engraved around the foot: *CHRISTOPH DOMEIGER.WE.MARIA. MAGDALENA.DESEN. EHLIBSTE* and inside the bowl: *v.braunschweig 1683*.

Beaker

Danish, probably Thyge
Pedersen (active 1618–*c.*1640),
Ribe, Denmark, dated 1637
Silver, height 7.8 cm
WA2013.1.103.3

MARKS: struck twice on the side of the body with *TP* conjoined, probably the maker's mark of Thyge Pedersen (Forssman 1955, no.24)

PROVENANCE: unrecorded

In the form of a wooden beaker made from staves with three applied bands. Engraved around the lip rim with a stylised foliate band. Inscribed around the middle: *POTUM SERVORUM BENEDIC DEUS ALME TUORUM 1637* (O Gracious God, bless the drink of thy servants) and a shield with the letter '*G*'; engraved inside with a bearded figure (Christ?) holding an orb, and a naked woman reclining with the inscription: *MEMENTO MORI HODE MIHI CRES TIBI* (Remember death: me today, you tomorrow).

Beaker

German, probably Bamberg
c. 1560–70
Silver, parcel-gilt, height 6 cm
WA2013.1.97.3

MARKS: struck under the base with a letter *B* probably for Bamberg (probably Rosenberg 1922, no. 1085) and an unidentified maker's mark, *WE* conjoined; with an assay scape and engraved with the initials *CS*

PROVENANCE: unrecorded

Drum-shaped beaker, the body engraved with scrollwork and roundels with busts of a man in armour and a fashionably dressed woman. The lip rim is engraved with moresques with an applied reeded band below. Set on a stepped foot with three feet, each in the form of an angel with spread wings.

37 Spoons

Sometimes called a universal luxury, a silver spoon was often given as a christening or wedding gift. It was often the only item of any value that a person might own. Before the advent of matching table cutlery in the late seventeenth century, most people carried their own personal spoon and knife with them. The Wellby Bequest contains a rich and varied collection of spoons from across Northern Europe that range in date from the fourteenth to the late seventeenth centuries. MW

Spoon

Attributed to the Quick workshop, Barnstaple, *c.* 1630
Silver-gilt, length 17.8 cm
WA2013.1.74

MARKS: struck with an obscured hallmark in the bowl

PROVENANCE: unrecorded

LITERATURE: cf. Kent (1992) p. 170, no. B4c

The bowl is egg-shaped, engraved with foliage and has an elaborately cast and chased stem. The finial is in the form of a female bust. Pricked on the reverse of the bowl is *AL* above *IM*.

Combined folding spoon and fork

Swiss, Neuchâtel, attributed to Daniel Bullot (d. 1630), 1591
Silver-gilt, length 15 cm
WA2013.1.86.5

MARKS: Maker's mark *DB*, attributed to Daniel Bullot, d. 1630 (Neuchâtel 1993, p.61). The arms are those of the Chambrier family of Neuchâtel

PROVENANCE: unrecorded

With a three pronged fork and a detachable egg-shaped bowl. The handle is hinged and has a finial in the form of the head and torso of a naked woman. The back of the bowl is engraved with a shield of arms, flanked by the letters P and C and with 91 below.

Spoon

Norwegian, Bergen, by Gierdt Frølich (active 1596–1603), *c.* 1608–15
Silver, parcel-gilt
length 15 cm
WA2013.1.38.1

MARKS: struck on the back of the stem with a crowned B for Bergen (Krohn-Hansen & Kloster, 1957, p. 346) and maker's mark *GF*, for Gierdt Frølich (Krohn-Hansen & Kloster, 1957, p. 61)

PROVENANCE: unrecorded

LITERATURE: Krohn-Hansen & Kloster (1957) p. 61, pl. 21

The large slightly oval bowl is engraved inside with a heart pierced with two arrows, foliage, IHS in a circle and the inscription: SCHVR OLLESEN BERTE OLLE DOTTER 1·6·15 (Schur Ollesen, Berte, Olle's daughter, 1615). The back of the bowl is engraved with IHS conjoined. The engraved handle is flat and the finial is in the form of a covered cup.

Spoon

German or Swiss, sixteenth or early seventeenth century
Maplewood, silver, parcel-gilt
length 14.7 cm
WA2013.1.86.4

UNMARKED

PROVENANCE: unrecorded

LITERATURE: cf. Lösel (1983) pls. 157, 159 & 168; cf. Marquardt (1997) no. 93

Carved fig-shaped bowl on a short, flanged stem. Engraved silver mounts with acorn-shaped finial.

Combined folding spoon and fork with pen, toothpick and ear scoop

German, probably *c.* 1600
Silver-gilt, length 19 cm
WA2013.1.139

UNMARKED

PROVENANCE: unrecorded

LITERATURE: Literature: cf. Rosenberg (1925) no. 4017dd; cf. Tait (1991) nos 48 & 49; cf. London (2007) nos 60 & 61

Two-pronged fork, elaborately cast and chased, with high relief ornament including St George rescuing a praying princess from the dragon, winged putti, a siren and cherubs' heads. The prongs of the fork fit into a silver-gilt bowl, through the shoulders of a winged harpy. The bowl is engraved with foliate ornament. The finial unscrews and contains a pen, a toothpick, and an ear scoop.

Spoon (Polyeder Knopp)

Danish, Malmö (now Sweden)
by Rasmus Hansen (active 1574–1587), *c.* 1580
Silver, parcel-gilt
length 13.4 cm
WA2013.1.39.1

MARKS: struck on the back with the town mark of Malmö and maker's mark of Rasmus Hansen

PROVENANCE: unrecorded

LITERATURE: cf. Axel-Nilsson (1967); cf. Marquardt (1997) no. 75

Large round bowl with a short stem and icosahedron finial. Engraved with a ribbon inside the bowl.

38 Tobacco box

Northern European
mid-seventeenth century
Silver, parcel-gilt
length 6.8 cm
WA2013.1.244

UNMARKED

PROVENANCE: unrecorded

Oval box embossed and chased on the hinged lid with a battle scene and on the base with Perseus and Andromeda. On the sides are trophies of arms, putti and a scrolling cartouche with a letter, perhaps *D*. The inside of the lid is engraved with a woman in a landscape playing the flute.

The deeply modelled scenes on the lid and base of this box are *tours de force* of the embosser's craft. The highly-skilled goldsmith would have created them by repeatedly hammering a sheet of silver from behind onto a bed of soft chaser's pitch to push out the metal in high relief (embossing or *repoussé*). The depressions created would have then been filled with more pitch. Once the pitch was dry the panel would have been turned over and worked from the front. The modelling would then have been sharpened and finer details added using small chisel-like tools (chasing). The pitch prevents the deep modelling from crumpling and cracking while being chased. The entire process would have taken many hours and at certain stages the silver would have to be annealed by heating and rapid cooling to stop it becoming too brittle. Once complete, the pitch would have been melted and removed. The result is an astonishingly sculptural object, a miniature Baroque masterpiece made to fit in the palm of the hand. The sources of the scenes remain untraced. The base shows the story of Perseus and Andromeda. In Greek mythology, Andromeda, the daughter of the Aethiopian king Cepheus, was chained to a rock as a sacrifice to the sea monster Cetus. However, she was rescued by Perseus, who, riding the winged horse Pegasus, turned the monster to stone by showing it the severed head of Medusa (see also no. 30). MW

39 Cup with *Tomyris and Cyrus*

German, Nuremberg, by Johann Jacob Wolrab, 1662–4
Silver, parcel-gilt
height 26 cm
diameter 23.6 cm
WA2013.1.268

MARKS: struck on the rim with *N* for Nuremberg, as used 1660–4 (Tebbe *et al.* 2007, BZ22); maker's mark of J. J. Wolrab (Tebbe *et al.* 2007, MZ 996) struck on rim and foot; later French control mark on rim and foot

PROVENANCE: Baron Lionel de Rothschild, M.P. (by 1862); Leopold de Rothschild; Sotheby's, Geneva, 9 May 1988, lot 251

LITERATURE: Chaffers and Robinson (1863) no. 6135; Jones (1907) pl. XXXIV; Rosenberg (1922–8) 4247 (d) and (e) (both referring to this object); Tebbe *et al.* (2007), I, I, pp. 464–5, no. 2

In the centre of the shallow cup is a medallion depicting the Victory of Tomyris over Cyrus; on the left a soldier holds up Cyrus's decapitated head. In the background, in very low relief, Tomyris, in a tent decorated with a crowned *T*, places the head in a pot of blood (see p. 9). The stem is formed as the figure of Tomyris, again placing Cyrus's head in the pot. The remainder of the surface of the cup is embossed and chased with flowers. Around the foot are four silver plaques representing the animals of Africa, America, Europe, and Asia (figs 18–21).

Tomyris was Queen of the Massagetae. According to Herodotus, when King Cyrus invaded her lands she proclaimed; 'Since you are so insatiate for blood, I will give you your fill of it'. In the ensuing battle, Cyrus was defeated and killed. Tomyris sought out his head and placed it in a wineskin filled with blood, to fulfil her promise.

Johan Jacob Wolrab, an immigrant to Nuremberg, became a Master in the city's Goldsmiths' Guild in 1662. This is a virtuoso example of his early work. He was, as well as a goldsmith, an engraver of coin-dies and seals. He died in 1690. TW

Figs 18–21 Details of no. 39 showing the animals representing Africa, America, Europe, and Asia

40 Marriage casket (*knottekistje*)

Dutch, Hoorn, probably Reyndert Bel, 1664
Silver with gilt handle and lock escutcheon and key
height 9.4 cm
WA2013.1.227

MARKS: struck with the crowned lion rampant for the province of Holland and the crowned hunting horn for Hoorn (Voet 1982, p. 26, no. 4), the date letter A for 1664 (Voet 1982, p. 27) and the maker's mark a bell attributed to Reyndert Bel (Citroen 1993, p. 121)

PROVENANCE: unrecorded

LITERATURE: cf. Frederiks (1958) pp. 126–8

Rectangular casket with arched lid, supported on four plain ball feet. The lock escutcheon, key, and handle are elaborately cast and gilt. The sides and lid are finely engraved with scenes taken from the Old Testament. These include: on the front, Susannah and the Elders; the right hand side, Joseph and Potiphar's wife; the left hand side, the Sacrifice of Isaac; on the back, the Finding of Moses; two oval panels on the lid show Lot and his Daughters and the Triumph of David.

In the Dutch provinces of Holland and Friesland small silver marriage caskets were filled with coins and presented by men to their prospective brides when they proposed. If the gift was accepted the couple were considered formally engaged. Such caskets were known as *knottenkistjes* (knot caskets) because they arose out of the earlier custom of presenting the coins in a knotted cloth. In some cases the caskets were used to present specially made marriage medals.

This beautifully engraved example was made in Hoorn, then a prosperous port in West Friesland and an important base for the Dutch East India Company. It is struck with the maker's mark depicting a bell which is generally accepted to be the mark of Reyndert Bel, a highly skilled silversmith and engraver. Bel is first recorded working as a silversmith in Hoorn in 1657 and by 1676 he was Dean of the Goldsmiths' Guild. His work is rare but other similarly decorated caskets by him are in the Rijksmuseum, Amsterdam and the Westfries Museum, Hoorn. As on this casket, many of the Old Testament scenes on his work are derived from prints in the *Icones Biblicae* published by Matthäus Merian the Elder in the 1620s (see no. 26). MW

41 Coconut cup

German, perhaps Augsburg
c. 1650–1700
Coconut shell, silver
parcel-gilt
height 30 cm
WA2013.1.208

UNMARKED

PROVENANCE: unrecorded

LITERATURE: Fritz (1983) no. 221A and cf. no. 157 (example in Vienna)

The coconut shell is carved with three panels of Bacchanalian putti. It is mounted as a cup and cover in silver, partly gilt and partly patinated black; three hinged straps are formed as overlapping leaves. The stem is formed as a black man (intended as an Indian?), wearing a skirt and a turban-like head-dress, with bow and arrows. The head is fixed to the support of the coconut with three coarse nuts and bolts, probably a repair. The foot and lid have embossed flowers and fruit in patinated silver. The ball finial may be a replacement.

For the uses of coconuts as Kunstkammer objects, see no. 8. TW

Fig. 22 Detail of no. 41

42 Ruby glass tankard and pair of flasks

The technique of rendering small quantities of gold into tiny particles (colloidal gold) in the body of glass, producing a brilliant deep red, was a discovery of seventeenth-century alchemists. It was developed by Johann Rudolf Glauber (1604–1670) and by Johann Kunckel (*c.* 1637–1703), especially while Kunckel was working for the Elector of Brandenburg. From about 1684 ruby glass was manufactured in at least one glass house in southern Germany, but the exact location remains to be identified. TW

Tankard and cover

The glass probably southern Germany, the mounts Nuremberg, by Andreas Berckmann, *c.* 1685
Ruby glass, silver-gilt hinged lid and mounts
height 20.5 cm
WA2013.1.271

MARKS: the lid marked with the *N* town mark for Nuremberg as used 1681–5 (Tebbe *et al.* 2007, no. BZ26) and maker's mark *ABN* above a female figure holding a crescent (Tebbe *et al.* 2007, no. MZ56); makers' mark on foot mount

PROVENANCE: Sotheby's, London, 23 Feb. 1976, lot 166

LITERATURE: Kerssenbrock-Krosigk (2001) no. 226; Tebbe *et al.* (2007) I, I, p. 50, no. 24; cf. Schroder (2012) pp. 299–349

The thumbpiece and handle have applied angelic figures. The flask is surmounted by a pinecone finial. The lid is etched with three emblematic scenes with inscriptions in Latin and approximate translations in German: (1) a tower flanked by clouds, inscribed *NOCEAT TIBI NILQ PERICLI* (let no danger harm you) and *Dass uns kein Angst und Sturm wirdt schäd* (that no worry or storm harm us); (2) two hearts with a wing above and rainclouds, inscribed *SED TE TEGAT ALA POTENTIS* (but may the wing of the powerful one cover you) and *Sein flüger deck uns früe und spätt* (may his wings cover us soon and late); (3) a tree with a Jehovah symbol with rays, inscribed *ITA CRESCAS DANTE JEHOVA* (thus may you grow by God's gift) and *Gottlose uns wachsen durch sein Gnade* (may God let us grow through his mercy).

Two ribbed flasks

The glass probably southern Germany, the mounts Augsburg, by Tobias Baur, *c.* 1690–1710
Ruby glass, silver-gilt mounts
height 19 cm each

WA2013.275.1 and 2013.1.275.2

MARKS: on each, pinecone mark for Augsburg; maker's mark *TB* for Tobias Baur (Seling and Singer 2007, no. 1810)

PROVENANCE: unrecorded

LITERATURE: cf. Kerssenbrock-Krosigk (2001) nos 307–16; cf. Schroder (2012) no. 97

43 Niello beaker and cover

Russian, Moscow, *c.* 1690
Silver, parcel-gilt, niello
height 16.5 cm
WA2013.1.272

UNMARKED

PROVENANCE: unrecorded

LITERATURE: cf. von Solodkoff (1981) pls 93–101; cf. Dresden (2012) pp. 230–5

Beaker and cover nielloed with cartouches, foliate scrolls, flowers and birds. The stepped cover has a pierced pear-shaped finial that opens in six segments like a pomander (see no. 35). The beaker stands on three ball and claw feet. On a circular band beneath the base is a Russian inscription, translated by Michael Wellby as 'He who empties me once is a happy man. He who does it twice is a fool'.

Niello is a black compound of silver, copper, or lead sulphides that is pressed into engraved lines on a metal surface – usually silver, copper, or gold. Once fired in a furnace, ground off and polished this produces a durable grey/black surface that contrasts dramatically with the surrounding metal. Known since Antiquity, the technique remained popular in Russia long after its use had declined elsewhere in Europe. The craft reached its peak in sixteenth- and seventeenth-century Moscow. Although unmarked this beautiful beaker was probably made in the Imperial Workshops in the Kremlin. It clearly shows the influence of the Greek jewellers who had arrived there from Constantinople in the 1660s. They introduced Turkish techniques and intricate patterns that incorporate plants, flowers, fruit, and animals. Moscow remained the centre of the niello technique even after the capital was moved to St Petersburg in 1703. MW

44 Carved sleeve for a tankard

Probably German or Austrian
c. 1650–80
Elephant ivory
height 18.5 cm
WA2013.1.277

UNMARKED

PROVENANCE: A. Joseph, London; his sale, Christie's, London, 21–4 February 1871, lot 528; Wareham; Col. Long; sold Christie's London, 11 July 1895, lot 130; O. Landauer

LITERATURE: cf. Berliner (1928); Philippovich (1982) fig. 192 (as by Matthias Loth)

Sleeve, finely carved from part of a large ivory tusk, with gods and nymphs carousing and making music. On one side is a quartered shield of arms, with an inescutcheon beneath three helms, a coronet, and three crests; these are the arms of the Austrian family of von Auersperg, counts of the Holy Roman Empire (fig. 23).

Ivory carving was a luxury art form especially favoured at the courts of the German-speaking world in the seventeenth century. Ivory was valued for its rarity and exoticism and for the possibility it offered for fine carving.

This sleeve is of a kind made to form the sides of a large precious metal tankard or flagon. The first owner of what must have been a sumptuous object may possibly have been Count Wolf Engelbert von Auersperg (1610–1673).

Discreetly inscribed beneath the seat of the stool are the initials *ML*, presumably those of the carver. Michael Wellby believed these initials to be for Matthias Loth (1675–1738). However, the carving does not resemble that of other ivory carvings signed by or attributed to Loth and looks too early in style to be by him. TW

Fig. 23 View of no. 44 showing the arms of the Austrian von Auersperg family

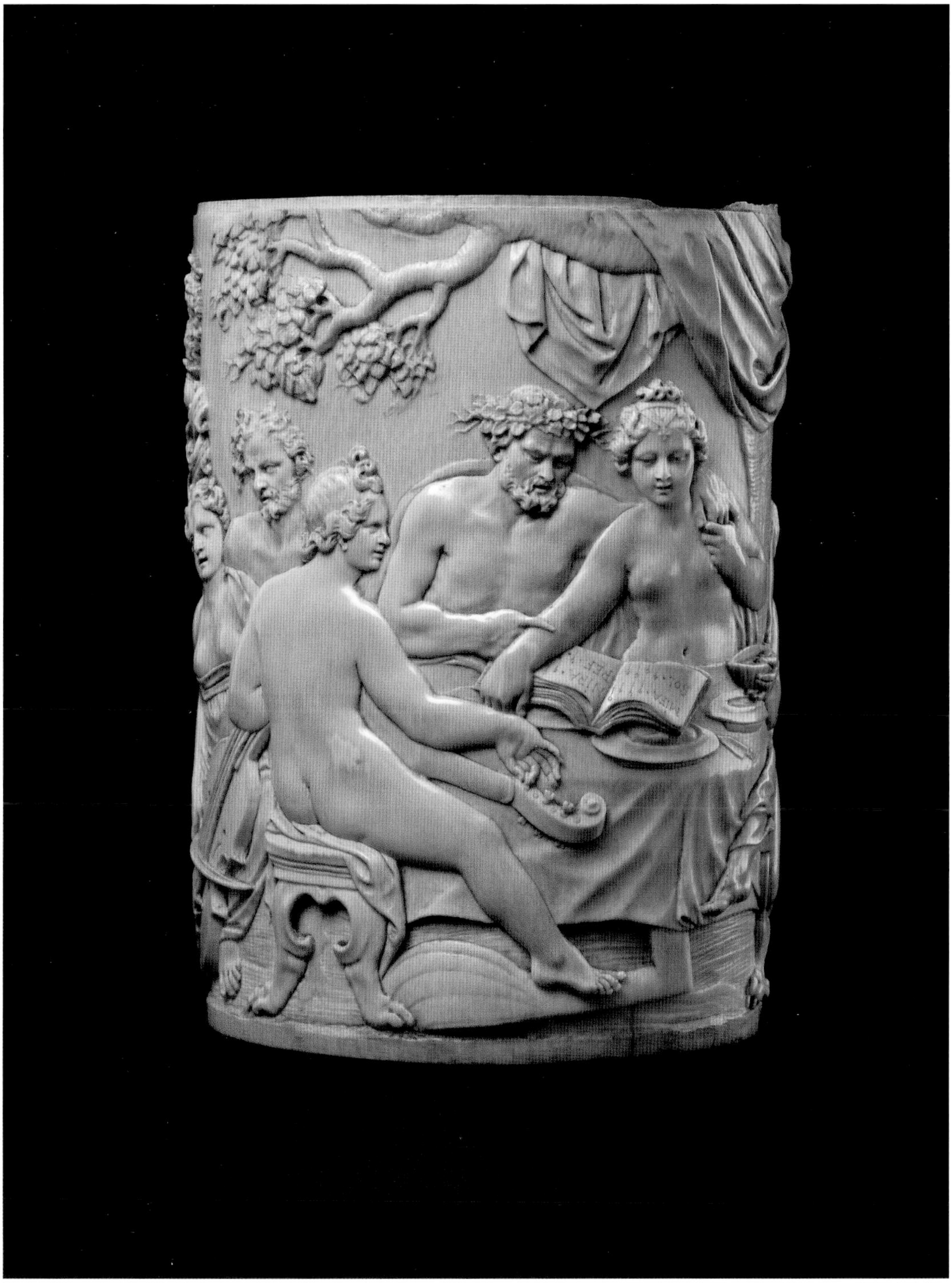

45 Beaker and cover

German, probably Dresden
c. 1720–50
Elephant ivory, silver-gilt and diamonds
height 24 cm
WA2013.1.303

UNMARKED

PROVENANCE: unrecorded

The ivory beaker is elaborately carved with scenes of a stag-hunt with horsemen and dogs. The lid is carved with a finial consisting of two dogs attacking a stag and, around the edge, stag-heads and dog-heads. The lining is of silver-gilt and the mounts of silver-gilt set with diamonds. The state of conservation is exceptional for so fragile an object.

Dresden was a great centre in the seventeenth and eighteenth century for the carving and lathe-turning of ivory; the Electors of Saxony were active patrons and collectors. Michael Wellby attributed this virtuoso example of carving to Johann Heinrich Köhler (1669–1736), who was court jeweller to Augustus the Strong at Dresden from 1716. This mounted beaker is indeed of the astonishing technical quality of objects that Köhler supplied to the court. However, it is not certain that Köhler was himself an ivory carver and the identity of the talented carver of this beaker remains to be discovered. TW

Fig. 24 View of the reverse of no. 45

46 Pair of plaques

Enamel saucers, German, Augsburg, probably by Johann Aufenwerth, *c.* 1705–10; mother-of-pearl and silver-gilt frames probably German, Augsburg, *c.* 1720–30
Painted enamel on copper, mother-of-pearl, silver-gilt, gold, 31 x 41 cm
WA2013.1.302.1–2

UNMARKED

PROVENANCE: Sotheby's, London, 4 July 1983, lot 260

LITERATURE: Weinhold (2000) no. 91; cf. London (2004) no. 398; cf. Galerie Georges Petit (1911) no. 85

Each lozenge-shaped plaque is set with a pair of enamel saucers painted with battle scenes after Georg Philipp Rugendas (1666 1742) and floral borders incorporating oval vignettes portraying allegories of the Four Elements, the Four Times of the Day, and classical gods and goddesses. The surrounding frames are entirely veneered with small pieces of carved and engraved mother-of-pearl. Each plaque has chased silver-gilt mounts with allegorical figures probably representing Victory and Peace, trophies of European and Turkish arms, and branches of oak. WA2013.302.1 shows a helmeted female figure holding a sword and flaming torch and a putto with a trumpet and laurel wreath (see pp. 20–1) while WA2013.302.2 shows a female figure holding a flail and shield, and a putto with a drum and palm frond. On the reverse, the engraved mother-of-pearl is arranged in elaborate geometrical designs.

Although the painted enamel saucers are without question early eighteenth-century Augsburg work, the extraordinary mother-of-pearl plaques into which they are set have prompted more debate. While some scholars have suggested that they are nineteenth-century, their fine quality and coherence of design probably indicate an earlier, eighteenth-century date. In Augsburg at that time highly-skilled craftsmen, known as *Silberkistlern*, specialised in supplying the courts of Europe with luxury objects made of mother-of pearl, ivory, and tortoiseshell. With their battle scenes, figures of Victory and Peace, and trophies of European and Turkish arms, these plaques appear to commemorate Austria's recent victories over the Turks in Hungary and the Balkans which finally halted Turkish expansion westwards. They recall a remarkable jewellery casket in the British Royal Collection that was made by Augsburg *Silberkistler* Emanuel Eichel in 1737. Made from tortoiseshell, mother-of-pearl, ivory, and gold, it commemorates Prince Eugen of Savoy's victories in the Austro-Turkish War of 1716–18. MW

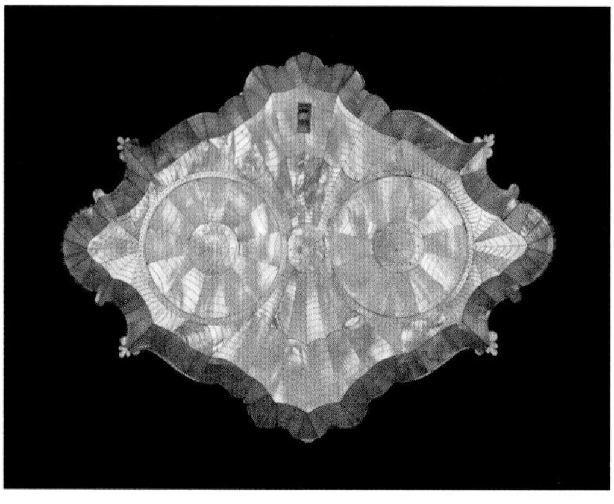

Fig. 25 Reverse of WA2013.1.302.1

47 Standing cup and cover

German, probably Augsburg
c. 1745–50
Silver, parcel-gilt
height 33.5 cm
WA2013.1.329

UNMARKED

PROVENANCE: unrecorded

LITERATURE: cf. Seling (1982) II, pl. 1002

The tiered bowl and cover are embossed and chased with hunting scenes and allegories of the arts and sciences within architectural *capricci* and asymmetrical *rocaille* and scrollwork. The domed cover is surmounted by a *commedia dell'arte* figure in a floppy ruff, cape and baggy hat playing a lute. The stem and foot are formed as a miner among his tools, surrounded by further *rocaille* work and scrolls.

Almost certainly made in Augsburg during the 1740s, this cup is a *tour de force* of rococo design and virtuoso technique. The stem and lid have been almost entirely raised from flat silver to form fully three-dimensional figures within swirling *rocaille* work and asymmetrical scrolls. It is a final flourish in the long tradition of great standing cups and covers that stretches back to the Middle Ages. The distinctive tiered shape of the cup is essentially a sixteenth-century form that has been brought up to date with the use of rococo ornament and the highly sculptural stem and lid. By the eighteenth century such cups tended to be reserved for ceremonial use only. A similar cup, made by four Augsburg goldsmiths between 1745 and 1747, now in the Badisches Landesmuseum, Karlsruhe, was originally a shooting trophy presented to the Lahr Shooting Club by the Prince of Nassau-Saarbrücken.

The lack of hallmarks and the fine quality of this cup suggest that it was a masterpiece cup submitted by an apprentice or journeyman for entry into the Augsburg Goldsmiths' Guild (see no. 31). However, the iconography can perhaps be interpreted as the arts and sciences literally supported by the riches created from mining. The cup may therefore have been made for an important patron who was also a mine owner. MW

48 The Virgin of the Immaculate Conception

Mexican Mexico City, *c.* 1790
Silver, parcel-gilt
height 24.4 cm
WA2013.1.349

MARKS: marked on the base and on the drapery with a crowned *M* for Mexico City; *FRDA* for Antonio Forcada y la Plaza, Assayer, Mexico City, 1790–1818 and a flying eagle tax mark

PROVENANCE: unrecorded

LITERATURE: cf. New York (1990) nos 189–90

Cast silver figure of the Virgin of the Immaculate Conception standing on a crescent moon. She wears a billowing cloak and clasps her hands together in prayer. Her corona of stars is missing (indicated by a hole at the back of her neck). The circular base is raised in faceted tiers and embossed and chased with flowers, *rocaille* scrollwork and floral garlands.

Silver made in Mexico, or Nuevo España (New Spain) as it was then known, demonstrated a rich and imaginative mixture of Spanish, Creole, and native cultures. This remarkably fine figure of the Virgin clearly shows the influence of the Mexican baroque style that first emerged over a century earlier. It would have been made for a church or for private devotion. The crescent moon on which she stands is a reference taken from the New Testament, the Vision of St John the Evangelist (Revelation 12:1) of a 'woman clothed with the sun, with the moon under her feet, and on her head a crown of twelve stars'. The doctrine of the Immaculate Conception maintains that the Virgin was born free from original sin. Immaculist devotion was particularly popular in Spain and Latin America. Similar figures of painted and gilded wood were also made and carved ivory versions were imported from the Philippines. Distinctly Mexican features of this figure include the large earrings and necklace that she wears and the extraordinarily heavy weight of the cast silver figure. This reflects the abundance of natural silver deposits in Mexico, one of the principal reasons that it had been colonised by the Spanish in the early sixteenth century.

The silversmith who made this exceptional piece remains unknown but it is struck with an early version of the mark used by the Mexico City Assayer Antonio Forcada y la Plaza (*FRDA* rather than the more usual *FCRA*). MW

49 Coffee pot

Italian, Rome, by Giovacchino Belli (1756–1822), *c.* 1820
Silver-gilt, oxidised silver
height 28 cm
WA2013.1.351

MARKS: struck on the side of the foot with the Rome hallmark, 2nd title (889/1000), medium works, used 1815–70 (Donati, 1993, no. 627) and the maker's mark *GIIB* for Giovacchino Belli

PROVENANCE: unrecorded

LITERATURE: cf. Rome (1970) nos 118 & 120; cf. Sotheby's, Paris, 26 June 2013, lot 142; cf. Sotheby's, Paris, 8 November 2012, lot 13

Of neoclassical vase form with a cast spout formed as a triton playing a horn, and a cast handle of black oxidized silver formed as a greyhound with a gilded collar. The neck is fluted. Round the shoulder is an applied frieze of winged putti playing. The lower body is embossed and chased with a band of laurel leaves. It stands on a plain square foot.

One of only a handful of neoclassical pieces in the Wellby Bequest, this elegant coffee pot was made in the workshop of Giovacchino Belli. Belli was the leading Roman silversmith of his day who supplied the Vatican and high-ranking nobility of the city. His large and successful workshop had been established by his father Vincenzo Belli (1710–1787) who had moved to Rome from Turin in 1740. This coffee pot shows the fine design and superb quality for which Belli was renowned. The unusual handle in the form of a greyhound is made of silver that has been deliberately blackened so that it resembles bronze. It was perhaps inspired by ancient classical sculptures. In contrast, the spout in the form of a triton appears to have been derived from baroque fountain figures. MW

50 Ladle

John Robins
(active 1771–1831),
London, 1812–13
Silver-gilt
length 10.5 cm
WA2013.1.352

MARKS: struck in the bowl with maker's mark of John Robins and London hallmarks for 1812/13; later control mark

PROVENANCE: made for William Beckford; subsequent provenance unrecorded

LITERATURE: cf. London (2001) no.109

Formed as a shell on a curved stem with foliate ornament and on the finial a cinquefoil with a cross *flory*.

One of the few English objects in the Wellby Bequest, this extraordinary piece was made for William Beckford (1760–1844). Its pair is now in the National Museum of Scotland, Edinburgh. Beckford was the wealthiest man in England and a renowned collector, author, and aesthete. He filled Fonthill Abbey, his vast neo-gothic country house with a magnificent and unparalleled collection of Medieval, Renaissance and later works of art. Through his agent and confidant Gregorio Fellipe Franchi (1770–1828), Beckford commissioned a small group of precious objects from London goldsmiths that were ornamented with Renaissance motifs. Many of these were derived from Beckford's extensive collection of ornamental prints and drawings. This ladle is based on a 1539 engraving by German artist Heinrich Aldegraver (fig. 26). William Gibbs Rogers, a wood carver, later recalled that 'Mons Franchi, a man of taste ... would come into the carvers' workshop with a volume of Holbein or Aldegraver, select a spoon or handle, and have them executed as high as he could get talent to bring them'. The goldsmith John Robins has copied the stem of the spoon in the foreground of the engraving almost exactly, adding only the Hamilton cinquefoil and Latimer cross to the finial. This records Beckford's descent through his mother from the Earls of Abercorn and Dukes of Hamilton and from William, 1st Lord Latimer. However, the plain hinged bowl in Aldegraver's design has been replaced by a heavy cast shell bowl, quite unlike anything made in the sixteenth century. It is a remarkably heavy object and may have been made simply to be admired as a work of art rather than used. MW

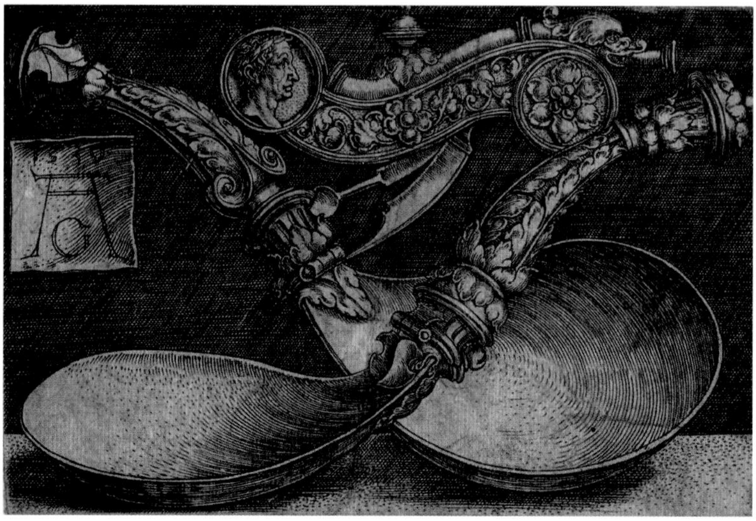

Fig. 26 Heinrich Aldegraver (1502–1558), *Design for two spoons and a dog whistle*, 1539. Engraving, 6.5 x 9.8 cm. British Museum, London, E,4.356 © The Trustees of the British Museum

Glossary

Auricular: literally 'in the form of an ear', describes the style, particularly associated with the Van Vianen family and their successors, creating abstract or fleshy forms that emphasize the ductility of the metal.

Basse-taille enamel: see no. 1.

Burnishing: polishing metal to a shine, for example with a hard smooth tool such as a piece of agate.

Cartouche: a decorative shield, often of scrolling form.

Caryatid: a column or pilaster formed wholly or partly as a female figure.

Champlevé: a technique in which coloured enamels are set within recessed areas in a metal surface and polished flat.

Chasing: the surface-working of metal, mainly from the front, without removal of metal.

Control mark: a mark struck on a precious metal object, often well after the date of manufacture, to indicate movement across borders or tax paid.

Credenza: the word may be used either of a service of silver or other tableware, or of the piece of furniture on which such a service is displayed; see p. 32.

Embossing: the working of metal by hammering from the back. Also known as *repoussé*.

Enamelling: a form of coloured glass applied to a metal surface and fused by firing. See *Champlevé, Basse-taille*.

Engraving: surface decoration of metal with a graver or burin, producing a v-shaped line.

Etching: surface decoration of metal, by scratching through a wax or similar coating, then applying acid, so that the exposed lines are 'bitten' by the acid.

Filigree: strands of metal bent and soldered into lace-like openwork patterns.

Fluting: shallow parallel concave grooves, as on a classical pillar.

Gadroons: convex ribs or curves.

Goldsmith: the term traditionally includes craftsmen working in silver or other precious materials.

Grotesques: a type of ornament, common from the Renaissance onwards, derived from ancient Roman wall-paintings and featuring fantastic creatures, fictive gems, etc. The word is derived from the Italian *grotta*, 'cavern', referring to the rooms of ancient Roman buildings which were discovered underground in the fifteenth century.

Gules: heraldic term for red.

Impaling: in heraldry, the placing of two shields of arms alongside each other within a single shield, often denoting a married couple.

Inescutcheon: a small shield placed usually in the centre of a shield of arms.

Journeyman: literally, a craftsman who is paid by the day; often referring to a goldsmith who has completed an apprenticeship but has not yet registered his own mark.

Kunstkammer: 'art chamber': more or less systematic assemblages of precious objects, works of art, and 'natural and artificial curiosities'. They were especially characteristic of princely collections on the Continent in the sixteenth and seventeenth centuries. See Introductory essay, pp. 15–19.

Maker's mark: a mark, specific to an individual goldsmith, composed of letters and/or symbols, struck on a piece of silver or gold; sometimes referred to as 'sponsor's mark'.

Master: a goldsmith who has completed an apprenticeship and registered his own mark as a member of the appropriate guild or company.

Masterpiece: An object made by a trainee goldsmith, usually on the completion of his apprenticeship, for submission to the appropriate guild or company to demonstrate his worthiness to be admitted as a member.

Memento mori: 'Remember that you must die' –a reminder of mortality to Christians.

Moresques: engraved or other decoration featuring scrolling stylised foliage, more or less closely derived from the ornament in Islamic (Moorish) art.

Mother-of-pearl: the iridescent and layered shell of certain marine molluscs.

Nef: a model ship used as a table decoration; see no. 29

Niello: see no. 43.

Parcel-gilt: gilt over part of the surface of an object.

Patinated: a surface effect, usually darker than the polished surface of the metal, on a copper-alloy or other metal object; it may have developed naturally over time or have been artificially applied.

Pax: a portable image, usually of the Crucifixion, passed round the congregation to be kissed during the Roman Catholic Mass.

Raising: the process of forming a metal vessel by hammering upwards, usually over a stake.

Rocaille: a form of ornament associated with the Rococo and composed of scroll work incorporating rock and shell motifs.

Rosary: a string of beads on which Roman Catholics count off prayers, including the Ave Maria and Pater Noster.

Ruby glass: see no. 42.

Salt: the traditional name for a salt cellar.

Strapwork: surface decoration imitating curled strips of leather applied to a surface, developed in sixteenth-century France and Italy.

Tazza: the normal Italian word for 'cup', which has come to be used in English silver parlance to describe a flattish cup or bowl on a stem.

Thumbpiece: a projecting element on the lid of a tankard or other vessel with a hinged lid, facilitating the lifting of the lid.

Bibliography

The Arundel Society for Promoting the Knowledge of Art, *Decorative Plate, chiefly Portuguese, German, and Italian* (London, 1869)

Atasoy, Nurhan, and Julian Raby, *Iznik: The Pottery of Ottoman Turkey* (London, second ed., 1994)

Axel-Nilsson, Av Göran, 'Om silverskedar med s.k. polyederknopp', *Röhsska konstslöjdmuseets årsbok* (Göteborg, 1967) pp. 8–21

Bachtler, Monika, *et al.*, *Die Faszination des Sammelns. Meisterwerke der Goldschmiedekunst aus der Sammlung Rudolf-August Oetker* (exh. cat., Dresden, 2011)

Berliner, Rudolf, 'Der Schnitzer Matthias Loth in München', in *Georg Habich zum zum 60. Geburtstag* (Munich, 1928) pp. 104–11.

Bock, Sebastian, *Ova struthionis: die Strausseneiobjeckte in den Schatz-, Silver- und Kunstkammern Europas* (Freiburg im Breisgau, Heidelberg, 2006)

Büttner, Andreas, *Perlmutt* (Petersberg, Germany, 2000)

Chaffers, William, and John Charles Robinson, 'Decorative Plate, chiefly of the 16th and 17th centuries, of various foreign origin', in ed., J. C. Robinson, *Catalogue of the Special Exhibition of Works of Art of the Mediaeval, Renaissance, and more recent periods on loan at the South Kensington Museum, June 1862* (London, 1863) pp. 501–41

Citroen, Karel, *Dutch Goldsmiths' and Silversmiths' Marks and Names Prior to 1812* (Leiden, 1993)

Von Hülsen-Esch, Andrea, and Hiltrud Westermann Angerhausen, Hiltrud, ed., *Zum Sterben schön. Alter, Totentanz und Sterbekunst von 1500 bis heute. Ausstellungskatalog* (exh. cat., Cologne, 2006)

Darcel, Alfred, 'L'orfèvrerie civile', in *La collection Spitzer* (Paris 1890–2) III, pp. 1–31

Distelberger, Rudolf, *Die Kunst des Steinschnitts* (exh. cat., Kunsthistorisches Museum, Vienna, 2002)

Donati, Ugo, *I marchi dell'argenteria italiana: oltre 1000 marchi territoriali e di garanzia dal XIII sealo a oggi* (Novara, 1993)

Dresden, *Die Faszination des Sammelns* (exh. cat., Residenzschloss, Dresden, 2011)

Dresden, *Zwischen Orient und Okzident. Schätze des Kreml von Iwan dem Schrecklichen bis Peter dem Grossen* (exh. cat., Residenzschloss, Dresden, 2012)

Falke, Otto von, *The Art Collection Eugen Gutmann* (Berlin, 1912)

Falke, Otto von, 'Der Augsburger Goldschmied Johannes Lencker', *Pantheon*, Bd. 1 (1928) p. 12f

Forrsman, Erik, *Anders Zorns Silversamling* (Stockholm, 1955)

Frederiks, J.W., *Dutch Silver III* (The Hague, 1958)

Fritz, Rolf, *Die Gefässe aus Kokosnuss in Mitteleuropa 1250–1800* (Mainz, 1983)

Fromanger, H. D., J. P. and V., and Jan Diviš, *Poinçons d'argent du monde entier* (Paris, 2004)

Galerie Georges Petit, *Orfèverie allemande, flamande, espagnole, italienne; pietra dures montées; noires et bois sculptées des XVe, XVIIe et XVIIIe siecles provenant de l'ancieene collection de feu M. Carl Mayer de Rothschild* (Paris, 1911)

Habich, Georg, *Die deutschen Schaumünzen des 16. Jahrhunderts* (Munich, 1929–34)

Hahnloser, Hans R. and Susanne Brugger-Koch, *Corpus der Hartsteinschliffe des 12.–15.* Jahrhunderts (Berlin, 1985)

Hasse, Max, *Lübecker Silber, 1480–1800, mit Katalog der Jubiläumausstellung 'Altes Lübecker Silber' 23. September bis 24. Oktober 1965* (Lübeck, 1965)

Hayward, John, *Virtuoso Goldsmiths and the Triumph of Mannerism* (London, 1976)

Hernmarck, Carl, *The Art of the European Silversmith 1430–1830* (London, 1977)

Hoyer, Eva Maria, *Sächsischer Serpentin. Ein Stein und seine Verwendung* (exh. cat., Grassimuseum, Leipzig, 1995)

Jones, E. Alfred, *Catalogue of the Collection of Old Plate of Leopold de Rothschild Esquire* (London, 1907)

Kent, Timothy, *West Country Silver Spoons and their Makers*, 1500–1750 (London, 1992)

Kerssenbrock-Krosigk, Dedo von, *Rubinglas des ausgehenden 17. und des 18. Jahrhunderts* (Mainz, 2001)

Kohlhaussen, Heinrich, *Nürnberger Goldschmiedekunst des Mittelalters und der Dürerzeit* (Berlin, 1968)

Koldeweij, Anna C, 'Van kunstkamer toto museumzaal; De nagelaten collective van Michael Wellby', *Vind Magazine* 17 (2015), Uitgeverij Polder Vondsten, pp. 32–7

Krautwurst, Miriam, *Reinhold Vasters – ein niederrheinischer Goldschmied des 19. Jahrhunderts in der Tradition alter Meister. Sein Zeichnungskonvolut im Victoria & Albert Museum, London* (Ph. D. thesis, University of Trier, 2003) Available online at http://ubt.opus.hbz-nrw.de/volltexte/2006/358/pdf/Reinhold_Vasters.pdf

Kris, Ernst, *Goldschmiedearbeiten des Mittelalters der Renaissance und des Barock. I. Arbeiten in Gold und Silber* (Vienna, 1932)

Lambacher, Lothar, 'Sceptrum quod vocatur Carolinum. Das sogenannte Zepter Karls des Großen aus der Abtei Werden im Berliner Kunstgewerbemuseum' in *Nicht die Bibliothek, sondern das Auge. Westeuropäische Skulptur und Malerei an der Wende zur Neuzeit, Beiträge zu Ehren von Hartmut Krohm, hg. von der Skulpturensammlung der Staatlichen Museen zu Berlin und Tobias Kunz* (St Petersberg, 2008) pp. 29–40

Lehfeldt, Prof. Dr. P. *Bau-und Kunst-Denkmäler Thüringens*, Bd. II, Heft IV (Jena, 1888)

London, *William Beckford, 1760–1844: An Eye for the Magnificent* (exh. cat., Dulwich Picture Gallery, London, 2001)

London, *George III and Queen Charlotte: Court Patronage and Taste* (exh. cat., The Queen's Gallery, Buckingham Palace, 2004)

Lösel, Eva-Maria, *Zürcher Goldschmeidekunst* (Zürich, 1982)

Luthmer, F, *Der Schatz des Freiherrn Karl von Rothschild. Meisterwerke alter Goldschmiedekunst aus dem 14.–18. Jahrhundert* (Frankfurt, 1883)

Mette, Hanns-Ulrich, *Der Nautiluspokal. Wie Kunst und Natur miteinander spielen* (Munich/Berlin, 1995)

Müller, Hannelore, *European Silver: the Thyssen-Bornemisza Collection* (London, 1986)

Neuchâtel, *Orfèvrerie neuchâteloise: du XVIIe au XXe sieécle* (exh. cat., Musée d'art et d'histoire, Neuchâtel, 1993)

New York, *Mexico: Splendors of Thirty Centuries* (exh. cat., Metropolitan Museum of Art, 1990)

Nijmegen, *Nijmeegs zilver* (exh. cat., Nijmegen, 1983)

Nuremberg, *Wenzel Jamnitzer und die Nürnberger Goldschmiedekunst 1500–1700* (exh. cat., Germanisches Nationalmuseum, Nuremberg, 1985)

Nys, Wim, *Zilveren wind- & waterenmolenbekers in Europa ca. 1530–1760* (Ghent, 2012)

Pazaurek, Gustav, *Perlmutter* (Berlin, 1937)

Pechstein, Klaus, *Goldschmiedewerke der Renaissance.* Kataloge des Kunstgewerbemueums Berlin, V (Berlin, 1971)

Philippovich, Eugen von, *Elfenbein* (second ed., Munich, 1982)

Pijzel-Dommisse, Jet, *Haags goud en zilver* (The Hague, 2005)

Rainer, Paulus, *et al.*, eds., *Splendour and Power. Imperial Treasures from Vienna* (exh. cat., Fitzwilliam Museum, Cambridge, 2011)

Randall, Richard, 'A group of gothic ivory boxes', *Burlington Magazine* 127 (1985) pp. 577–81

Read, Sir Hercules, and Tonnochy, A.B., *Catalogue of the silver plate, Mediaeval and later, bequeathed to the British Museum by Sir Augustus Wollaston Franks, with selected examples from other sources* (London, 1928)

Repton, John Adey, 'Oxnead Hall, Norfolk', *Gentleman's Magazine*, new series 21 (1844) pp. 22–4, 150–3

Richter, Ernst-Ludwig, *Altes Silber: Imitiert, Kopiert, Gefälscht* (Munich, 1983)

Richter, Ernst-Ludwig. 'Mauritz Kaltschmidt', *Weltkunst* 75 (2005) pp. 67–9

Robinson, John Charles, 'Various Objects of Mediaeval Art', in ed., J. C. Robinson, *Catalogue of the Special Exhibition of Works of Art of the Mediaeval, Renaissance, and more recent periods on loan at the South Kensington Museum, June 1862* (London, 1863) pp. 86–8

Rohrwasser, Alfred, *Edelmetall-Punzierung in Österreich von 1524 bis 1987* (Perchtoldsdorf, second ed., 1987)

Rome, *Argenti Romani di tre secoli nelle raccolte private* (exh. cat., Palazzo Braschi, Rome, 1970)

Rosenberg, Marc, *Der Goldschmiede Merkzeichen* (Berlin, third ed,. 1922–8)

Smollich, R., *Der Bisamapfel in Kunst und Wissenschaft* (Stuttgart, 1983)

Schiedlausky, G., 'Vom Bisamapfel zur Vinaigrette: Zur Geschichte der Duftgefässe' in *Kunst und Antiquitäten* 4 (1985) pp. 28–38

Scholten, Frits, *Willem van Tetrode Scupltor/Guglielmo Fiammingo scultore* (exh. cat., Rijksmuseum, Amsterdam, and Frick Collection, New York, 2003)

Schroder, Timothy, *The Gilbert Collection of Gold and Silver* (Los Angeles, 1988)

Schroder, Timothy, *Renaissance Silver from the Schroder Collection* (exh. cat., Wallace Collection, London, 2007)

Schroder, Timothy, *British and Continental Gold and Silver in the Ashmolean Museum* (Oxford, 2009)

Schroder, Timothy, *Renaissance and Baroque Silver, Mounted Porcelain and Ruby Glass from the Zilkha Collection* (London, 2012)

Seling, Helmut, *Die Kunst der Augsburger Goldschmiede 1529–1868* (Munich, 1980)

Seling, Helmut, *Die Kunst der Augsburger Goldschmiede 1529–1868 Supplement zu Band III* (Munich, 1994)

Seling, Helmut, and Stephanie Singer, *Die Augsburger Gold- und Silberschmiede 1529–1868* (Munich, 2007)

Solodkoff, Alexander von, *Russian Gold and Silver* (London, 1981)

Spitzer sale, *Catalogue des objets d'art et de haute curiosité... composant l'importante et précieuse collection Spitzer* (Paris, Chevallier, 17 April–16 June 1893)

Syndram, Dirk, and Antje Scherner, ed., *Princely Splendor: The Dresden Court 1580–1620* (exh. cat., Hamburg, New York, and Rome, 2004)

Tait, Hugh, *Catalogue of the Waddesdon Bequest in the British Museum. II. The Silver Plate* (London, 1988)

Tait, Hugh. *Catalogue of the Waddesdon Bequest in the British Museum. III. The 'Curiosities'* (London, 1991)

Tebbe, Karin *et al.*, *Nürnberger Goldschmiedekunst 1541–1868* (Nuremberg, 2007)

Ter Molen, Johannes, *Van Vianen: een Utrechtse familie van zilversmeden met een internationale faam* (Rotterdam, 1984)

Thompson, Eleanor, 'The Wellby Bequest: memories of Michael', *Silver Studies. The Journal of the Silver Society* 29 (2013) pp. 125–6

Truman, Charles, 'Oxford's silver-gilt bequest', *The Art Newspaper* 244 (March 2014) p. 26

Trusted, Marjorie, 'Maria Faydherbe: a seventeenth-century sculptor in Mechelen', *The Burlington Magazine* CLVI (2014) pp. 104–6

Utrecht, *Zeldzaam Zilver uit de Gouden Eeuw. De Utrechtse edelsmeden Van Vianen.* (exh. cat., Centraal Museum, Utrecht, 1984)

Van den Bergh-Hoogterp, Louise, and B. Dubbe, *De Verzamelingen van het Centraal Museum Utrecht. Edele en onedele metalen* (Utrecht, 1997)

Vassallo e Silva, Nuno, *Ourivesaria portuguesa de aparato séculos XV e XVI* (Lisbon, 2012)

Venturelli, Paola, *Il Tesoro dei Medici al Museo degli Argenti* (Florence, 2009)

Voet, Elias, *Nederlandse Goud- en Zilvermerken* (The Hague, 1970)

Voet, Elias, *Nederlandse Goud- en Zilvermerken* (Leiden, 1982)

Warren, Jeremy, *Medieval and Renaissance Sculpture in the Ashmolean Museum* (Oxford, 2014)

Weinhold, Ulrike, *Emailmalerie an Augsburger Goldschmeidearbeiten von 1650 bis 1750* (Berlin, 2000)

Weinhold, Ulrike, and Martina Minning, eds., *Zwischen Orient und Okzident. Schätze des Kreml von Iwan dem Schrecklichen bis Peter dem Grossen* (exh. cat., Dresden, 2012)

Wellby, Michael. *The Wellby Collection*. Draft catalogue, intended for private circulation but left incomplete at Michael Wellby's death in 2012

Williamson, Paul and Glyn Davies, *Medieval Ivory Carvings 1200–1550* (London, 2014)

Wilson, Timothy, 'The Michael Wellby Bequest', *The Ashmolean* 65 (spring 2013), pp. 3–5

Wilson, Timothy. 'The Wellby Room', *The Ashmolean* 69 (spring 2015), pp. 8–9

Wodehouse, Katherine, ed., *The Ashmolean Museum: Crossing Cultures, Crossing Time* (Oxford, 2014)

Index

Museums are indexed under the place where they are located. Towns are normally indexed under their modern names.